VISUAL BASIC S

Edition 2

By

Dr.Liew

Disclaimer

Visual Basic Sample Code Edition 2 is an independent publication and is not affiliated with, nor has it been authorized, sponsored, or otherwise approved by Microsoft Corporation.

Trademarks

Microsoft, Visual Basic, Excel, Access and Windows are either registered trademarks or trademarks of Microsoft Corporation in the United States and/or other countries. All other trademarks belong to their respective owners.

Liability

The purpose of this book is to provide a basic guide for people interested in Visual Basic programming. Although every effort and care has been taken to make the information as accurate as possible, the author shall not be liable for any error, harm or damage arising from using the instructions given in this book.

Copyright © 2013 Liew Voon Kiong

All rights reserved. No Part of this e-book may be reproduced, in any form or by any means, without permission in writing from the author.

About the Author

Dr. Liew Voon Kiong holds a bachelor's degree in Mathematics, a master's degree in management and a doctoral degree in business administration. He has been involved in programming for more than 15 years. He created the popular online Visual Basic Tutorial at www.vbtutor.net in 1996 and since then the web site has attracted millions of visitors and it is one of the top searched **Visual Basic Tutorial** websites in many search engines including Google. To provide more support for the Visual Basic hobbyists, he has written this book based on the online Visual Basic tutorial.

Preface

The sample programs in this book were developed using Visual Basic 6. However, they can be easily modified to build applications for VB.Net. Visual Basic 6 is a third-generation event-driven programming language first released by Microsoft in 1991. In Visual Basic 6, the sky's the limit. You can develop all kinds of applications, including educational apps, financial apps, games, multimedia apps, animations, database applications and more.

Visual Basic 6 Samples Code comprises 290 pages of captivating content and 48 fascinating sample codes. All the examples are explained in great details using easy-to-understand language and illustrated with gorgeous Images.

By reading the book and using the sample source codes, you will master Visual Basic programming effortlessly!

You will be able to:

·   Understand basic to intermediate concepts of Visual Basic programming.

·   Create your own Visual Basic 6 programs from scratch.

·   Get programming ideas from 48 interesting sample programs.

·   Modify the source codes easily to suit your needs.

Table of Contents

Preface 3

Table of Contents...4

1. Games and Fun 1

    1.1 Simple Animated Slot Machine 1

    1.2 Advanced Animated Slot Machine 5

    1.3 Professional Casino Slot Machine................................12

    1.4 Dice 22

    1.5 Jigsaw Puzzle 25

    1.6 Memory Game 29

1.7 Passwords Cracking Program...33

    1.8 Reversi 39

    1.9 Snakes and Ladders Game...70

    1.10 Star War Game...87

    1.11 Tic Tac Toe 96

    1.12 Time Bomb...106

    1.13 Lucky Draw 109

    1.14 Boggle..111

2. Educational Programs..113

    2.1 Kid's Math...113

    2.2 Pythagorean Theorem..125

    2.3 Factors Finder 127

    2.4 Prime Number Tester 129

2.5 Geometric Progression..131

2.6 Maximum Number Calculator 133

2.7 Quadratic Equation Solver 135

2.8 Quadratic Graph Plotter......................................138

2.9 Simultaneous Equations Solvers...........................140

2.10. The Sine Rule 144

2.11 Projectile..147

2.12 Simple Harmonic Motion 149

3. Financial Programs 151

3.1 Amortization Calculator 151

3.2 Depreciation Calculator.......................................154

3.3 Future Value Calculator.......................................156

3.5 Payback Period Calculator...................................161

4. Graphics Programs 163

4.1 Drawing Pad 163

5 Multimedia Programs 173

5.1 Creating a DVD Player 175

5.2 A Smart Audio Player 178

5.3 Multimedia Player 185

6 Tools and Utilities 191

6.1 BMI Calculator 191

6.2 Calculator 193

6.3 Digital Clock 203

6.4 Polling System...204

6.5 Digital Stopwatch..207

6.6 Choice Selection Program...214

7 Database Applications..216

7.1 Simple Database Management System 216

7.2 A Simple Database Application 220

7.3 A Library Management System 224

7.4 Inventory Management System 246

8. Internet Applications...266

8.1 Web Browser 266

8.2 FTP Program 272

Index 281

1. Games and Fun
1.1 Simple Animated Slot Machine

This simple slot machine was created using Visual Basic 6. While it does not exactly resemble the real machines played in casinos, it does demonstrate the concept of randomness and probability in an actual slot machine. Slot machine is a game of chance; many different outcomes will appear when the player presses the play button.

In this program, you need to draw an array of nine shapes ,Visual Basic will automatically label the shapes as shape1(0), shape1(1), shape1(2), shape1(3), shape1(4), shape1(5), shape1(6), shape1(7) and shape1(8) respectively. Arrange the shapes into three rows. Write the code so that only three types of shapes appear randomly. The shapes are square, oval and rectangle. Their appearance can be set at runtime using the Shape properties. For example, Shape1 (0).Shape=0 means it is a rectangle, Shape1 (0).Shape=1 is a square and Shape1 (0).Shape=2 is an oval shape. The colors of the shapes are controlled by the FillColor property of the shapes. For example, Shape1(0).FillColor=vbRed will give the shape a red color. Besides, the default FillStyle property is transparent; therefore, you need to set the FillStyle property to solid so that the colors can show up.

Randomness can be achieved by using the Rnd function. You must also insert a timer to create the animated effect of the slot machine. The time interval is set to 10 so that the shapes change at a fast rate to create the illusion of animation. The program also uses a variable x to control the timer so that it can be stopped when x attains a specific value, otherwise the program will loop forever. The purpose of this program is just to show how different shapes can appear randomly, therefore many advanced features of a slot machine such as the amount of bet are not included here.

The design UI us shown in Figure 1.1

The Design UI

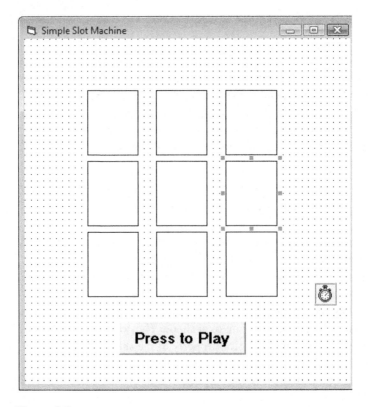

Figure 1.1

The Runtime IUI is as shown in Figure 1.2

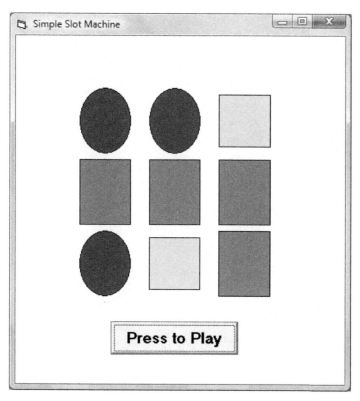

Figure 1.2

The code

Private Sub Command1_Click()

'To start the timer

Timer1.Enabled = True
x = 0

End Sub

Private Sub Timer1_Timer()

4

```vb
x = x + 10
Dim a, i As Integer
For i = 0 To 8

'To generate random integers 0,1 and 2
a = Int(Rnd * 3)
Shape1(i).Shape = a
Shape1(i).FillStyle = Solid
If a = 0 Then
Shape1(i).FillColor = vbRed
ElseIf a = 1 Then
Shape1(i).FillColor = vbGreen
Else
Shape1(i).FillColor = vbBlue
End If

Next i

'To stop the timer
If x > 500 Then
Timer1.Enabled = False
End If

End Sub
```

1.2 Advanced Animated Slot Machine

This is a more advanced animated slot machine created using Visual Basic 6, an improvement from the simple animated slot machine. The slot machine allows the player to enter the amount to bet. Besides that, we add sound and music to the program. The interface is shown in Figure 1.3

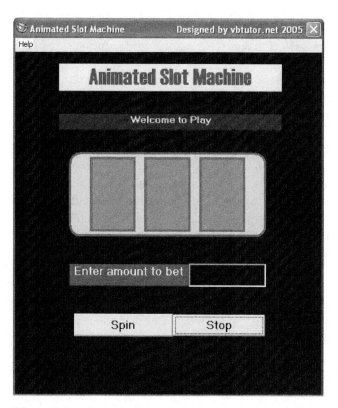

Figure 1.3

To design the UI, drag the form to a suitable size. Insert a Label control and place it at the top part of the part. Change its caption to **'Animated Slot Machine'**, set proper font type, font size as well as

6

foreground and background colors. Next, insert another Label control and place it immediately below the first Label. This Label serves as the display panel for showing the amount the user wins. The display will be animated.

Besides that, place a shape control and set its shape property to rounded rectangle. Drag it to a proper size and fill it with a suitable solid color. It will act as the background panel for the spinning shapes. Now for the spinning shapes, insert a shape control into the form and then copy and paste repeatedly to create a control array of three shapes, each will be identified by its index. The first is shape1(0), the second is shape1(1) and the third shape1(2).

Retain the default shape property as rectangle and only change their shapes during runtime. Place all the three shapes on top of the first shape control, use color to make the former shapes stand out. In addition, insert another Label below the shape controls above and change its caption to **'Enter amount to bet'** to give instruction to the player the amount to bet. To let the player enters the amount they want to bet, insert a text box on the right of the above label and clear its text. The next two controls you need to insert into the form are two command buttons, one of them you label its caption as "Spin" and the other one you label it as "Stop".

To create the animated effect, you must insert a timer and set its interval to 20, which is equivalent to 0.02 second. You must also set its **Enabled** property to False so that the slot machine will not start until the user presses the "Spin" button. Besides, you need to insert the Multimedia Control to produce the sound effects. To include the multimedia control as one of the controls, click on project on the menu in Visual Basic 6 IDE and select components, and then click on **Microsoft Multimedia Control 6.0** to add it to the Toolbox.

Once the Microsoft Multimedia Control icon is added to the Toolbox, you can add the Multimedia Control into your form. In this program, you need to use two Microsoft Multimedia Controls, one for playing the spinning sound and the other for the jackpot sound. You must set the **Visible** property of both Microsoft

7

Multimedia Controls to False so that they will not initiate at start-up. Last, insert a menu item and label it as "**Help**" and a submenu item and label it as "**Instruction**".

The code

```
Dim x As Integer

Dim amount As Integer

Dim a, b, c As Integer

Private Sub Spin_Click()

Timer1.Enabled = True

MMControl1.Command = "Close"

MMControl2.Command = "close"

x = 0

Label2.Caption = "Your Credits"

amount = Val(Text1)

End Sub

Private Sub Stop_Click()

End

End Sub

Private Sub Form_Click()

Label3.Visible = False

End Sub

Private Sub Form_Load()

Label1.Caption = " Welcome to Play"

Label3.Visible = False

End Sub
```

8

```vb
'To display instructions when the user clicks on the menu item Help
Private Sub instruct_click()
 Label3.Visible = True
End Sub

Private Sub Text1_Change()
amount = Val(Text1)
End Sub

Private Sub Timer1_Timer()
If x < 500 Then
spin
Else
Timer1.Enabled = False
MMControl1.Command = "Stop"
Label1.Alignment = 2
If (a = 3 And b = 3 And c <> 3) Or (a = 3 And c = 3 And b <> 3) Or _
 (b = 3 And c = 3 And a <> 3) Then
Label1.Caption = " You win 20 dollars"
amount = amount + 20
End If
If (a = 4 And b = 4 And c <> 4) Or (a = 4 And c = 4 And b <> 4) Or _
(b = 4 And c = 4 And a <> 4) Then
Label1.Caption = " You win 30 dollars"
amount = amount + 30
End If
If (a = 5 And b = 5 And c <> 5) Or (a = 5 And c = 5 And b <> 5) Or _
```

```vb
 (b = 5 And c = 5 And a <> 5) Then

Label1.Caption = " You win 40 dollars"

amount = amount + 40

End If

If (a = 3 And b = 3 And c = 3) Or (a = 4 And b = 4 And c = 4) Or _

 (a = 5 And b = 5 And c = 5) Then

'To play sound

MMControl2.Notify = False

MMControl2.Wait = True

MMControl2.Shareable = False

MMControl2.DeviceType = "WaveAudio"

MMControl2.FileName = "C:\ My Documents\VB
program\audio\jackpot.wav"

MMControl2.Command = "Open"

MMControl2.Command = "Play"

Label1.Caption = "Congratulation! Jackpot!!! You win 200 dollars!"

amount = amount + 200

End If

If (a = 3 And b = 4 And c = 5) Or (a = 3 And b = 5 And c = 4) _

Or (a = 4 And b = 3 And c = 5) Or (a = 4 And b = 5 And c = 3) _

Or (a = 5 And b = 4 And c = 3) Or (a = 5 And b = 3 And c = 4) Then

Label1.Caption = "Too bad, you lost 50 dollars"

amount = amount – 50

End If

If amount < 0 Then

Label1.Caption = "Oh! You're bankrupt!"
```

10

```vb
End If

Text1.Text = Str$(amount)

End If

End Sub

'To simulate spinning of the shapes

Sub spin()

x = x + 10

Randomize Timer

a = 3 + Int(Rnd * 3)

b = 3 + Int(Rnd * 3)

c = 3 + Int(Rnd * 3)

MMControl1.Notify = False

MMControl1.Wait = True

MMControl1.Shareable = False

MMControl1.DeviceType = "WaveAudio"

MMControl1.FileName = "C:\ My Documents\VB
program\audio\slot2.wav"

MMControl1.Command = "Open"

MMControl1.Command = "Play"

Label1.Caption = "Good Luck!"

Label1.Alignment = a - 3

Shape1(0).Shape = a

If a = 3 Then

Shape1(0).FillColor = &HFF00&

End If

If a = 4 Then
```

```
Shape1(0).FillColor = &HFF00FF
End If
If a = 5 Then
Shape1(0).FillColor = &HFF0000
End If
Shape1(1).Shape = b
If b = 3 Then
Shape1(1).FillColor = &HFF00&
End If
If b = 4 Then
Shape1(1).FillColor = &HFF00FF
End If
If b = 5 Then
Shape1(1).FillColor = &HFF0000
End If
Shape1(2).Shape = c
If c = 3 Then
Shape1(2).FillColor = &HFF00&
End If
If c = 4 Then
Shape1(2).FillColor = &HFF00FF
End If
If c = 5 Then
Shape1(2).FillColor = &HFF0000
End If
End Sub
```

12

1.3 Professional Casino Slot Machine

This a slot machine that resembles the real slot machines in the casinos. To design the UI, insert three image boxes into the form and write code so that they will display a set of three different pictures randomly when the user presses on the spin button. It involves a randomization process. Next, insert a timer and write relevant code to produce animated effects. In addition, insert the **Microsoft Multimedia Control** so that it can play sounds that synchronize with the spinning of the slot machine as well as when the player hits the jackpot.

Next, declare three variables a, b and c that will be randomly assigned the values of, 2 and 3 using the **Rnd** function. Based on these three random numbers, three different images will be loaded into the three image boxes randomly using the **LoadPicture** method. Animated effects are created by entering the procedure under the control **Timer1**, which will call the **spin** procedure after every interval until it fulfills a certain condition, as shown below:

```
Private Sub Timer1_Timer()

'Call the spin procedure

spin
.......The rest of the code......

End Sub
```

The spin procedure

```
Sub spin()

a = 3 + Int(Rnd * 3)

b = 3 + Int(Rnd * 3)

c = 3 + Int(Rnd * 3)
.......The rest of the code....
```

End Sub

Sounds are added using the Microsoft Multimedia Control to make the game more exciting and interesting. The amount won is controlled by the **If...Then** statements, illustrated as follows:

If (a = 3 And b = 3 And c <> 3) Or (a = 3 And c = 3 And b <> 3) Or _

(b = 3 And c = 3 And a <> 3) Then

Label1.Caption = " You win 20 dollars"

amount = amount + 20

End If

It is important that you define the correct path for the LoadPicture method; otherwise the program will fail to load the images. For example, our path is **C:\VB program\Images\grape.gif**, you need to create the necessary folders and have the necessary image file if you wish to copy the program directly. If you place the image file in a differently folder, you need to modify the path accordingly. For example, if your image file is in D:\VB program\Images\grape.gif, then you need to modify the LoadPicture method to **LoadPicture ("D:\VB program\Images\grape.gif")**.

The UI is show in Figure 1.4.

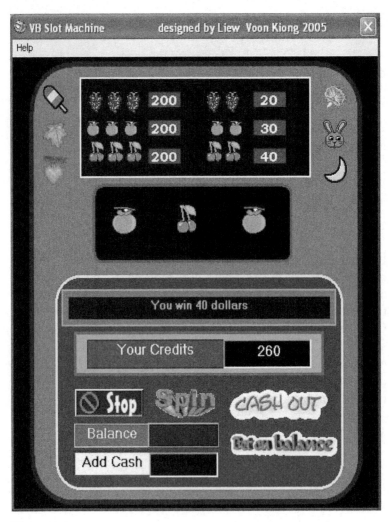

Figure 1.4

15

The code

```vb
Dim x As Integer

Dim amount As Variant

Dim balance As Variant

Dim a, b, c As Integer

Private Sub Command1_Click()

End

End Sub
```

'Code for the Bet on balance button

```vb
Private Sub betbal_Click()

Label13.Caption = Str$(Val(Label6.Caption) + Val(Label13.Caption))

Label6.Caption = ""

End Sub
```

'Code for the Cash Out button

```vb
Private Sub Cashout_Click()

If Val(Label13.Caption) > 0 Then

balance = Val(Label6.Caption) + Val(Label13.Caption)

Label13.Caption = ""

Label6.Caption = Str$(balance)

Label1.Caption = "Please bet again"

Else

Label1.Caption = "Sorry, you have no money to cash out."

End If

End Sub
```

16

```
Private Sub Form_Click()

Label3.Visible = False

End Sub

Private Sub Form_Load()

Label1.Caption = " Welcome to Play"

Label3.Visible = False

Image1(0).Picture = LoadPicture("C:\My Documents\VB &_
program\Images\grape.gif")

Image1(1).Picture = LoadPicture("C:\My Documents\VB &_
program\Images\cherry.gif")

Image1(2).Picture = LoadPicture("C:\ My Documents\ VB &_
program\Images\orange.gif")

End Sub
```

'To show instruction on a label control

```
Private Sub instruct_click()

Label3.Visible = True

End Sub

Private Sub Label12_Click()

Label13.Caption = Str$(Val(Label13.Caption) + Val(Text2.Text))

Text2.Text = ""

End Sub
```

'The spin procedure

```
Private Sub spin_Click()

Timer1.Enabled = True

MMControl1.Command = "Close"
```

17

```vb
MMControl2.Command = "close"
x = 0
amount = Val(Text1)
balance = Val(Label6)
End Sub
```

'Code for the Spin button

```vb
Private Sub spining_Click()
If Val(Label13.Caption) > 0 Then
Timer1.Enabled = True
MMControl1.Command = "Close"
MMControl2.Command = "close"
x = 0
amount = Val(Label13.Caption)
balance = Val(Label6)
Else
Label1.Caption = "Sorry, you have no money to spin, add cash."
End If
End Sub
```

'To stop the game

```vb
Private Sub stop_Click()
End
End Sub

Private Sub Timer1_Timer()
```

'Call the spin procedure

```vb
spin
```

18

```
x = x + 20
If x > 500 Then
Timer1.Enabled = False
MMControl1.Command = "Stop"
Label1.Alignment = 2
If (a = 3 And b = 3 And c <> 3) Or (a = 3 And c = 3 And b <> 3) Or _
(b = 3 And c = 3 And a <> 3) Then
Label1.Caption = " You win 20 dollars"
amount = amount + 20
End If
If (a = 4 And b = 4 And c <> 4) Or (a = 4 And c = 4 And b <> 4) Or _
(b = 4 And c = 4 And a <> 4) Then
Label1.Caption = " You win 30 dollars"
amount = amount + 30
End If
If (a = 5 And b = 5 And c <> 5) Or (a = 5 And c = 5 And b <> 5) Or _
(b = 5 And c = 5 And a <> 5) Then
Label1.Caption = " You win 40 dollars"
amount = amount + 40
End If
If (a = 3 And b = 3 And c = 3) Or (a = 4 And b = 4 And c = 4) Or_
(a = 5 And b = 5 And c = 5) Then
'Playing sound
MMControl2.Notify = False
MMControl2.Wait = True
MMControl2.Shareable = False
```

```vb
MMControl2.DeviceType = "WaveAudio"
MMControl2.FileName = "C:\My Documents\VB _
program\audio\jackpot.wav"
MMControl2.Command = "Open"
MMControl2.Command = "Play"
Label1.Caption = " Congratulation! Jackpot!!! You win 200 dollars!"
amount = amount + 200
End If
If (a = 3 And b = 4 And c = 5) Or (a = 3 And b = 5 And c = 4) Or _
(a = 4 And b = 3 And c = 5) Or (a = 4 And b = 5 And c = 3) Or _
(a = 5 And b = 4 And c = 3) Or (a = 5 And b = 3 And c = 4) Then
Label1.Caption = " Too bad, you lost 100 dollars"
amount = amount - 100
End If
If amount < 0 Then
Label1.Caption = "Oh! you're bankrupt! Add cash to play!"
End If
Label13.Caption = Str$(amount)
End If
End Sub
'The spin sub procedure
Sub spin()
a = 3 + Int(Rnd * 3)
b = 3 + Int(Rnd * 3)
c = 3 + Int(Rnd * 3)
```

20

```vb
MMControl1.Notify = False

MMControl1.Wait = True

MMControl1.Shareable = False

MMControl1.DeviceType = "WaveAudio"

MMControl1.FileName = "C:\ My Documents\VBprogram\audio\slot2.wav"

MMControl1.Command = "Open"

MMControl1.Command = "Play"

Label1.Caption = "Good Luck!"

Label1.Alignment = a - 3

If a = 3 Then

Image1(0).Picture = LoadPicture("C:\ My Documents\VB _
program\Images\grape.gif")

End If

If a = 4 Then

Image1(0).Picture = LoadPicture("C:\ My Documents\VBprogram\ _
Images\cherry.gif")

End If

If a = 5 Then

Image1(0).Picture = LoadPicture("C:\My Documents\VBprogram\ _

Images \orange.gif")

End If

If b = 3 Then

Image1(1).Picture = LoadPicture("C: \ My Documents\VBprogram\_
Images\grape.gif")

End If

If b = 4 Then
```

21

```
Image1(1).Picture = LoadPicture("C:\ :\ My Documents\VBprogram\ _
Images \cherry.gif")

End If

If b = 5 Then

Image1(1).Picture = LoadPicture("C:\ My Documents\VBprogram\_

 Images  \orange.gif")

End If

If c = 3 Then

Image1(2).Picture = LoadPicture("C:\ My Documents\VBprogram\_

Images grape.gif")

End If

If c = 4 Then

Image1(2).Picture = LoadPicture("C:\ My Documents\VBprogram\_

 Images \cherry.gif")

End If

If c = 5 Then

Image1(2).Picture = LoadPicture("C:\ :\ My Documents\VBprogram\ _
Images \orange.gif")

End If

End Sub
```

1.4 Dice

This program creates a dice that can be used to play board games. Indeed, it can also be incorporated into any VB game that requires a die. Example of games that require the use of a dice is step and ladder game, monopoly, boggle, Backgammon and more.

To design the UI, the first step is to draw a rounded square in the project windows. Secondly, you need to draw an array of seven dots using the shape control. VB will automatically label them as shape1(0), shape1(1), shape1(2), shape1(3), shape1(4), shape1(5) and shape1(6). You can control the appearance of the dots using the random function **Rnd**. Each time the user clicks the 'Roll' button, he or she can see different combinations of dots. The UI is as shown in Figure 1.5

Figure 1.5

The Code

```
Private Sub Command1_Click()

n = Int(1 + Rnd * 6)

For i = 0 To 6

    Shape1(i).Visible = False

Next

If n = 1 Then

    Shape1(3).Visible = True

    Shape2.FillColor = &HC0C0C0

End If

If n = 2 Then

    Shape1(2).Visible = True

    Shape1(4).Visible = True

    Shape2.FillColor = &H8080FF

End If

If n = 3 Then

    Shape1(2).Visible = True

    Shape1(3).Visible = True

    Shape1(4).Visible = True

    Shape2.FillColor = &H80FF&

 End If

If n = 4 Then

    Shape1(0).Visible = True

    Shape1(2).Visible = True

    Shape1(4).Visible = True
```

```
    Shape1(6).Visible = True
    Shape2.FillColor = &HFFFF00
 End If
If n = 5 Then
   Shape1(0).Visible = True
   Shape1(2).Visible = True
   Shape1(3).Visible = True
   Shape1(4).Visible = True
   Shape1(6).Visible = True
   Shape2.FillColor = &HFFFF&
 End If
 If n = 6 Then
   Shape1(0).Visible = True
   Shape1(1).Visible = True
   Shape1(2).Visible = True
   Shape1(4).Visible = True
   Shape1(5).Visible = True
   Shape1(6).Visible = True
   Shape2.FillColor = &HFF00FF
 End If
End Sub
```

1.5 Jigsaw Puzzle

Jigsaw puzzle is a game that requires the player to fix back the pieces of a picture that were cut into pieces and jumbled up. There are many levels of difficulties, some are easy whereas some are difficult.

You can create a simple 3x3 jigsaw puzzle using Visual Basic 6. You may program it in such a way that you can drag and drop the pieces in the squares that you think are correct. If the piece is correct, it will stay in the correct square otherwise it will not stay there. The UI is as shown in Figure 1.6

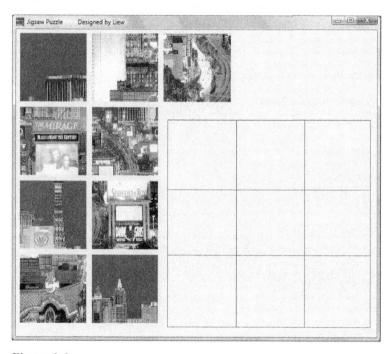

Figure 1.6

The code

```
Dim imgindex As Integer

Dim imgtag As String

Private Sub Image1_DragDrop(Index As Integer, Source As Control, X As Single, _

Y As Single)

imgtag = Source.Tag

imgindex = Index

Select Case imgindex

Case 0

If imgtag = "11" Then

    Image1(0).Picture = Image1(9).Picture

    Source.Visible = False

Else

Source.Visible = True

End If

Case 1

If imgtag = "12" Then

    Image1(1).Picture = Image1(10).Picture

    Source.Visible = False

Else

Source.Visible = True

End If

Case 2

If imgtag = 13 Then

    Image1(2).Picture = Image1(11).Picture
```

```
        Source.Visible = False
Else
Source.Visible = True
End If
Case 3
If imgtag = 21 Then
    Image1(3).Picture = Image1(12).Picture
    Source.Visible = False
Else
Source.Visible = True
End If
Case 4
If imgtag = 22 Then
    Image1(4).Picture = Image1(13).Picture
    Source.Visible = False
Else
Source.Visible = True
End If
Case 5
If imgtag = 23 Then
    Image1(5).Picture = Image1(14).Picture
    Source.Visible = False
Else
Source.Visible = True
End If
```

28

```vb
Case 6
If imgtag = 31 Then
    Image1(6).Picture = Image1(15).Picture
    Source.Visible = False
Else
Source.Visible = True
End If
Case 7
If imgtag = 32 Then
    Image1(7).Picture = Image1(16).Picture
    Source.Visible = False
Else
Source.Visible = True
End If
Case 8
If imgtag = 33 Then
    Image1(8).Picture = Image1(17).Picture
    Source.Visible = False
Else
Source.Visible = True
End If
End Select
End Sub
```

1.6 Memory Game

This is a typical memory game for children. The user must click the rectangles to reveal the hidden pictures and if the two pictures are matched, they will disappear together. He or she wins the game when all the pictures are cleared.

In this program, you need to add an array of twelve image controls and twelve picture boxes to the form and cover the images with the picture boxes. To match the images, you can use tags to identify them; same image should be given the same tag. The tags are being set at the images' properties windows. When two picture boxes covering the images is being clicked, the program checks for the tags of the images and if found that they are the same, then they become invisible. The UI is as shown in Figure 1.7

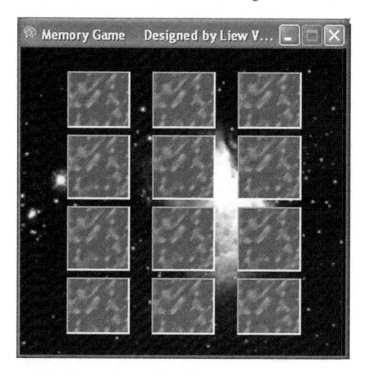

Figure 1.7

30

The code

```vb
Sub check()
'Check whether the images are the same or not
For i = 0 To 11
If Picture1(i).Visible = False Then
For j = 0 To 11
If Picture1(j).Visible = False Then
If i <> j And Image1(i).Tag = Image1(j).Tag Then
Image1(j).Visible = False
Image1(i).Visible = False
Picture1(j).Visible = False
Picture1(i).Visible = False
End If

If i <> j And Image1(i).Tag <> Image1(j).Tag And Image1(i).Visible = True And _ Image1(j).Visible = True Then
Picture1(j).Visible = True
Picture1(i).Visible = True
End If
End If
Next j
End If
Next i
Timer1.Enabled = False
```

```vb
If Picture1(0).Visible = False _
And Picture1(1).Visible = False _
And Picture1(2).Visible = False _
And Picture1(3).Visible = False _
And Picture1(4).Visible = False _
And Picture1(5).Visible = False _
And Picture1(6).Visible = False _
And Picture1(7).Visible = False _
And Picture1(8).Visible = False _
And Picture1(9).Visible = False _
And Picture1(10).Visible = False _
And Picture1(11).Visible = False _
Then
MMControl1.Notify = False
MMControl1.Wait = True
MMControl1.Shareable = False
MMControl1.DeviceType = "WaveAudio"
MMControl1.FileName = "D:\Liew Folder\VB
program\audio\applause.wav"
MMControl1.Command = "Open"
MMControl1.Command = "Play"
End If
End Sub
```

32

```
Private Sub picture1_Click(Index As Integer)
Picture1(Index).Visible = False
Timer1.Enabled = True
End Sub


Private Sub Timer1_Timer()
check
End Sub
```

1.7 Passwords Cracking Program

This is a password cracking program that can generate possible passwords and compares each of them with the actual password. If the generated password found to be equal to the actual password, login will be successful. The UI is as shown in Figure 1.8

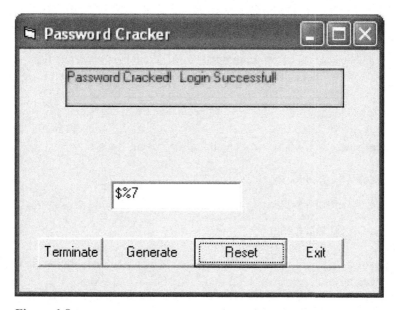

Figure 1.8

In this program, you need to add three timers to the form. Next, enter the passwords generating code under each of the Timer ( ) event by double-clicking the relevant timer. The interval of the timers can be set in their properties window. An interval value of 1 is equivalent to 1 millisecond, and a value of 1000 is 1 second: the smaller the value, the shorter the interval. The Timer's Enabled property is set to False so that the program will only start generating the passwords after the user clicks on the command button.

You can generate random passwords by using the **Rnd** function. **Rnd** is a Visual Basic function that generates a random number between 0 and 1. **Int** is a Visual Basic function that returns an integer by ignoring the decimal part of that number. For example, Int(Rnd * 255) returns an integer between 0 and 255.

This program only deals with three-character passwords to make the code simpler so that every reader can grasp the concept easily. To generate the alphanumeric characters, you can use the **Chr** function. The **Chr** function returns the string that corresponds to an ASCII code. For example, Chr(65)=A and Chr(37)=%. There are altogether 255 characters. The program needs to generate the characters for each of the characters in the passwords and compare them with the corresponding character in the password entered by the user. To achieve the purpose, you need to declare three integers, namely code1, code2 and code 3, respectively. Each of the integers will generate ASCII codes between 0 and 255 using the syntax

```
code1 = Int(Rnd * 255)
code2 = Int(Rnd * 255)
code3 = Int(Rnd * 255)
```

Besides that, you need to declare three strings; p1 to denote the first character of the password, p2 to denote the second character of the password and p3 to denote the third character of the password. You can then use the **Chr** function to find the corresponding alphanumeric character from randomly generated ASCII codes using the following syntax:

```
p1 = Chr(code1)
p2 = Chr(code2)
p3= Chr(code1)
```

After generating the characters, the program compares them to the characters of the actual password using the following syntax:

```
If Chr(code1) = Left(password, 1) Then

    p1 = Chr(code1)

If Chr(code2) = Mid(password, 2, 1) Then

p2 = Chr(code2)

If Chr(code3) = Right(password, 1) Then

    p3 = Chr(code3)
```

In addition, the program uses If…Then…Else to check whether the generated password is equal the actual password or not using the following syntax:

```
Text1.Text = p1 & p2 & p3
```

If they are equal, the passwords generating process will be terminated by setting the **Timer1.Enabled** property to False.

The Code

```
Dim password As String * 3

Dim crackpass As String

Dim p1, p2, p3 As String

Dim code1, code2, code3 As Integer

Dim x As Integer

Sub checkstatus()

Text1.Text = p1 & p2 & p3

If Text1.Text = password Then

Label1.Visible = True

Label1.Caption = "Password Cracked!  Login Successful!"

Else
```

36

```vba
Text1.Text = Chr(code1) + Chr(code2) + Chr(code3)

Label1.Visible = True

Label1.Caption = "Generating passwords, please wait...."

End If

End Sub

Private Sub Command1_Click()

Timer1.Enabled = True

Timer2.Enabled = True

Timer3.Enabled = True

End Sub

Private Sub Command2_Click()

Text2.Visible = False

Label2.Visible = False

Command2.Visible = False

password = Text2.Text

End Sub

Private Sub Command3_Click()

Label1.Visible = False

Text2.Visible = True

Label2.Visible = True

Command2.Visible = True

Text2.Text = ""

Text1.Text = ""

End Sub

Private Sub Command4_Click()
```

```
Timer1.Enabled = False
Timer2.Enabled = False
Timer3.Enabled = False
Text1.Text = ""
Label1.Caption = "Please try again"
End Sub

Private Sub Command5_Click()
End
End Sub

Private Sub Timer1_Timer()
 code1 = Int(Rnd * 255)
If Chr(code1) = Left(password, 1) Then
   p1 = Chr(code1)
Timer1.Enabled = False
Else
checkstatus
 End If
checkstatus
End Sub

Private Sub Timer2_Timer()
code2 = Int(Rnd * 255)
If Chr(code2) = Mid(password, 2, 1) Then
   p2 = Chr(code2)
Timer2.Enabled = False
Else
```

```
checkstatus

 End If

checkstatus

End Sub

Private Sub Timer3_Timer()

 code3 = Int(Rnd * 255)

If Chr(code3) = Right(password, 1) Then

   p3 = Chr(code3)

Timer3.Enabled = False

Else

checkstatus

 End If

 checkstatus

 End Sub
```

1.8 Reversi

This is the mini version of the typical reversi game. The program uses two sets of two-dimensional arrays (4x4) and declare them as Boolean , one represents the white piece and the other one represents the black piece. If a white piece or a black piece occupies a square, the variable becomes True, otherwise it is False.

Using this concept, the program can check how many white and black pieces appear on the reversi board and the positions they occupy. The program uses If...Then and Select Case... End Select statements to check for conditions whether a white piece or a black piece can be placed in a certain position so that the pieces trapped in between will change color. You can also add a procedure to display the number of white pieces and the number of black pieces at any one time and the name of the winner.

To design the interface, you need to insert an image control and then copy and paste the image repeatedly to form a 4x4 array of images. Each image is defined by its index. For example, Image1 (0) is the first image Image1 (1) is the second image, Image1(2) is the third image and so on. The positions of the images are shown in Table 1.1

Table 1.1

Image1(12)	Image1(13)	Image1(14)	Image1(15)
Image1(8)	Image1(9)	Image1(10)	Image1(11)
Image1(4)	Image1(5)	Image1(6)	Image1(7)
Image1(0)	Image1(1)	Image1(2)	Image1(3)

Next, you need to create two images, a white solid circle, and a black solid circle, save them as jpeg files. Load them into two image controls on the form. You can use whatever name for the two images, we used image17 to denote the while solid circle and image18 to denote the black circle. The two images are particularly important as you will later use the dragdrop method to enable the user to drag and drop the images into the circles. The UI is as shown in Figure 1.9

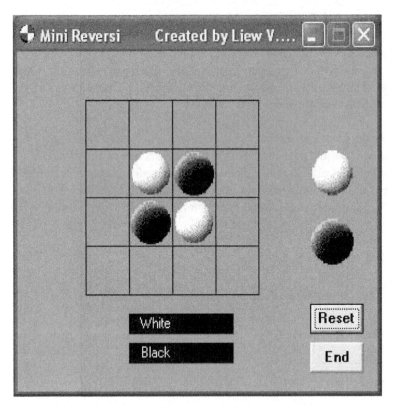

Figure 1.9

41

The Code

```vb
Option Base 1

Dim white(4, 4) As Boolean

Dim black(4, 4) As Boolean

Dim i, j, k, w, b As Integer

Dim imgtag As String

Private Sub Command1_Click()

'To reset the game

Label3.Caption = ""

Label4.Caption = ""

Label5.Visible = False

For m = 0 To 15

Image1(m).Picture = LoadPicture("")

Next m

Image1(5).Picture = Image18.Picture

Image1(10).Picture = Image18.Picture

Image1(9).Picture = Image17.Picture

Image1(6).Picture = Image17.Picture

Checkstatus

End Sub

Private Sub Command2_Click()

End

End Sub


Private Sub Form_Load()
```

```vb
Label5.Visible = False

Image1(5).Picture = Image18.Picture

Image1(10).Picture = Image18.Picture

Image1(9).Picture = Image17.Picture

Image1(6).Picture = Image17.Picture

End Sub

Private Sub Image1_DragDrop(Index As Integer, Source As Control, X
As Single, Y As Single)

imgtag = Source.Tag

checkstatus

'To  check whether image1(0)is destination of dragdrop and make sure
it is empty

If Index = 0 And black(1, 1) = False And white(1, 1) = False Then

Select Case imgtag

Case "white"

'Check row

If black(2, 1) = True And white(3, 1) = True Then

Image1(0).Picture = Image17.Picture

Image1(1).Picture = Image17.Picture

End If

If black(2, 1) = True And black(3, 1) = True And white(4, 1) = True Then

Image1(0).Picture = Image17.Picture

Image1(1).Picture = Image17.Picture

Image1(2).Picture = Image17.Picture

End If
```

```
'check diagonal
If black(2, 2) = True And white(3, 3) = True Then
Image1(0).Picture = Image17.Picture
Image1(5).Picture = Image17.Picture
End If
If black(2, 2) = True And black(3, 3) = True And white(4, 4) = True Then
Image1(0).Picture = Image17.Picture
Image1(5).Picture = Image17.Picture
Image1(10).Picture = Image17.Picture
End If
'Check column
If black(1, 2) = True And white(1, 3) = True Then
Image1(0).Picture = Image17.Picture
Image1(4).Picture = Image17.Picture
End If
If black(1, 2) = True And black(1, 3) = True And white(1, 4) = True Then
Image1(0).Picture = Image17.Picture
Image1(4).Picture = Image17.Picture
Image1(8).Picture = Image17.Picture
End If
Case "black"
If white(2, 1) = True And black(3, 1) = True Then
Image1(0).Picture = Image18.Picture
Image1(1).Picture = Image18.Picture
End If
```

```vb
If white(2, 1) = True And white(3, 1) = True And black(4, 1) = True Then
Image1(0).Picture = Image18.Picture
Image1(1).Picture = Image18.Picture
Image1(2).Picture = Image18.Picture
End If
If white(2, 2) = True And black(3, 3) = True Then
Image1(0).Picture = Image18.Picture
Image1(5).Picture = Image18.Picture
End If
If white(2, 2) = True And white(3, 3) = True And black(4, 4) = True Then
Image1(0).Picture = Image18.Picture
Image1(5).Picture = Image18.Picture
Image1(10).Picture = Image18.Picture
End If
'Check column
If white(1, 2) = True And black(1, 3) = True Then
Image1(0).Picture = Image17.Picture
Image1(4).Picture = Image17.Picture
End If
If white(1, 2) = True And white(1, 3) = True And black(1, 4) = True Then
Image1(0).Picture = Image17.Picture
Image1(4).Picture = Image17.Picture
Image1(8).Picture = Image17.Picture
End If
End Select
End If
```

```vb
'To compute the probabilities for position (2,1)
If Index = 1 And black(2, 1) = False And white(2, 1) = False Then
checkstatus
Select Case imgtag
Case "white"

If black(3, 1) = True And white(4, 1) = True Then
Image1(1).Picture = Image17.Picture
Image1(2).Picture = Image17.Picture
End If
If black(3, 2) = True And white(4, 3) = True Then
Image1(1).Picture = Image17.Picture
Image1(6).Picture = Image17.Picture
End If
If black(2, 2) = True And white(2, 3) = True Then
Image1(1).Picture = Image17.Picture
Image1(5).Picture = Image17.Picture
End If
If black(2, 2) = True And black(2, 3) = True And white(2, 4) = True Then
Image1(1).Picture = Image17.Picture
Image1(5).Picture = Image17.Picture
Image1(9).Picture = Image17.Picture
End If
Case "black"
If white(3, 1) = True And black(4, 1) = True Then
Image1(1).Picture = Image18.Picture
```

```
Image1(2).Picture = Image18.Picture

End If

If white(3, 2) = True And black(4, 3) = True Then

Image1(1).Picture = Image18.Picture

Image1(6).Picture = Image18.Picture

End If

If white(2, 2) = True And black(2, 3) = True Then

Image1(1).Picture = Image18.Picture

Image1(5).Picture = Image18.Picture

End If

If white(2, 2) = True And white(2, 3) = True And black(2, 4) = True Then

Image1(1).Picture = Image18.Picture

Image1(5).Picture = Image18.Picture

Image1(9).Picture = Image18.Picture

End If

End Select

End If

'To compute the position for (3,1)

If Index = 2 And black(3, 1) = False And white(3, 1) = False Then

Select Case imgtag

Case "white"

If black(2, 1) = True And white(1, 1) = True Then

Image1(1).Picture = Image17.Picture

Image1(2).Picture = Image17.Picture

End If
```

```
If black(2, 2) = True And white(1, 3) = True Then
Image1(2).Picture = Image17.Picture
Image1(5).Picture = Image17.Picture
End If

If black(3, 2) = True And white(3, 3) = True Then
Image1(2).Picture = Image17.Picture
Image1(6).Picture = Image17.Picture
End If

If black(3, 2) = True And black(3, 3) = True And white(3, 4) = True Then
Image1(2).Picture = Image17.Picture
Image1(6).Picture = Image17.Picture
Image1(10).Picture = Image17.Picture
End If

Case "black"
If white(2, 1) = True And black(1, 1) = True Then
Image1(1).Picture = Image18.Picture
Image1(2).Picture = Image18.Picture
End If
If white(2, 2) = True And black(1, 3) = True Then
Image1(2).Picture = Image18.Picture
Image1(5).Picture = Image18.Picture
End If

If white(3, 2) = True And black(3, 3) = True Then
Image1(2).Picture = Image18.Picture
```

```vb
Image1(6).Picture = Image18.Picture

End If

If white(3, 2) = True And white(3, 3) = True And black(3, 4) = True Then

Image1(2).Picture = Image18.Picture

Image1(6).Picture = Image18.Picture

Image1(10).Picture = Image18.Picture

End If

End Select

End If

'To compute position (4,1)

If Index = 3 And black(4, 1) = False And white(4, 1) = False Then

Select Case imgtag

Case "white"

If black(3, 1) = True And white(2, 1) = True Then

Image1(2).Picture = Image17.Picture

Image1(3).Picture = Image17.Picture

End If

If black(3, 1) = True And black(2, 1) = True And white(1, 1) = True Then

Image1(1).Picture = Image17.Picture

Image1(2).Picture = Image17.Picture

Image1(3).Picture = Image17.Picture

End If

If black(3, 2) = True And white(2, 3) = True Then

Image1(3).Picture = Image17.Picture

Image1(6).Picture = Image17.Picture
```

End If

If black(3, 2) = True And black(2, 3) = True And white(1, 4) = True Then

Image1(3).Picture = Image17.Picture

Image1(6).Picture = Image17.Picture

Image1(9).Picture = Image17.Picture

End If

If black(4, 2) = True And white(4, 3) = True Then

Image1(3).Picture = Image17.Picture

Image1(7).Picture = Image17.Picture

End If

If black(4, 2) = True And black(4, 3) = True And white(4, 4) = True Then

Image1(3).Picture = Image17.Picture

Image1(7).Picture = Image17.Picture

Image1(11).Picture = Image17.Picture

End If

Case "black"

If white(3, 1) = True And black(2, 1) = True Then

Image1(2).Picture = Image18.Picture

Image1(3).Picture = Image18.Picture

End If

If white(3, 1) = True And white(2, 1) = True And black(1, 1) = True Then

Image1(1).Picture = Image18.Picture

Image1(2).Picture = Image18.Picture

Image1(3).Picture = Image18.Picture

End If

```
If white(3, 2) = True And black(2, 3) = True Then
Image1(3).Picture = Image18.Picture
Image1(6).Picture = Image18.Picture
End If

If white(4, 2) = True And black(4, 3) = True Then
Image1(3).Picture = Image18.Picture
Image1(7).Picture = Image18.Picture
End If
If white(4, 2) = True And white(4, 3) = True And black(4, 4) = True Then
Image1(3).Picture = Image18.Picture
Image1(7).Picture = Image18.Picture
Image1(11).Picture = Image18.Picture
End If
If white(3, 2) = True And white(2, 3) = True And black(1, 4) = True Then
Image1(3).Picture = Image18.Picture
Image1(6).Picture = Image18.Picture
Image1(9).Picture = Image18.Picture
End If
End Select
End If

'To compute position (1,2)
If Index = 4 And black(1, 2) = False And white(1, 2) = False Then
Select Case imgtag
Case "white"
'Check row
```

```
If black(2, 2) = True And white(3, 2) = True Then

Image1(4).Picture = Image17.Picture

Image1(5).Picture = Image17.Picture

End If

If black(2, 2) = True And black(3, 2) = True And white(4, 2) = True Then

Image1(4).Picture = Image17.Picture

Image1(5).Picture = Image17.Picture

Image1(6).Picture = Image17.Picture

End If

'check column

If black(1, 3) = True And white(1, 4) = True Then

Image1(4).Picture = Image17.Picture

Image1(8).Picture = Image17.Picture

End If

'check diagonal

If black(2, 3) = True And white(3, 4) = True Then

Image1(4).Picture = Image17.Picture

Image1(9).Picture = Image17.Picture

End If

Case "black"

If white(2, 2) = True And black(3, 2) = True _

And black(2, 2) = False And white(3, 2) = False Then

Image1(4).Picture = Image18.Picture

Image1(5).Picture = Image18.Picture

End If
```

```vb
If white(2, 2) = True And white(3, 2) = True And black(4, 2) = True Then
Image1(4).Picture = Image18.Picture
Image1(5).Picture = Image18.Picture
Image1(6).Picture = Image18.Picture
End If
If white(1, 3) = True And black(1, 4) = True Then
Image1(4).Picture = Image18.Picture
Image1(8).Picture = Image18.Picture
End If

If white(2, 3) = True And black(3, 4) = True _
And black(2, 3) = False And white(3, 4) = False Then
Image1(4).Picture = Image18.Picture
Image1(9).Picture = Image18.Picture
End If
End Select
End If

'To compute position (4,2)
If Index = 7 And black(4, 2) = False And white(4, 2) = False Then
Select Case imgtag
Case "white"
'Check row
If black(3, 2) = True And white(2, 2) = True Then
Image1(6).Picture = Image17.Picture
Image1(7).Picture = Image17.Picture
End If
```

```
If black(3, 2) = True And black(2, 2) = True And white(1, 2) = True Then
Image1(5).Picture = Image17.Picture
Image1(6).Picture = Image17.Picture
Image1(7).Picture = Image17.Picture
End If

'check column
If black(4, 3) = True And white(4, 4) = True Then
Image1(7).Picture = Image17.Picture
Image1(11).Picture = Image17.Picture
End If

'check diagonal
If black(3, 3) = True And white(2, 4) = True Then
Image1(7).Picture = Image17.Picture
Image1(10).Picture = Image17.Picture
End If
Case "black"
If white(3, 2) = True And black(2, 2) = True Then
Image1(6).Picture = Image18.Picture
Image1(7).Picture = Image18.Picture
End If
If white(2, 2) = True And white(3, 2) = True And black(1, 2) = True Then
Image1(5).Picture = Image18.Picture
Image1(6).Picture = Image18.Picture
Image1(7).Picture = Image18.Picture
End If
```

```vb
If white(4, 3) = True And black(4, 4) = True Then
Image1(7).Picture = Image18.Picture
Image1(11).Picture = Image18.Picture
End If

If white(3, 3) = True And black(2, 4) = True Then
Image1(7).Picture = Image18.Picture
Image1(10).Picture = Image18.Picture
End If
End Select
End If
'To compute position (1,3)
If Index = 8 And black(1, 3) = False And white(1, 3) = False Then
Select Case imgtag
Case "white"
'Check row
If black(2, 3) = True And white(3, 3) = True Then
Image1(8).Picture = Image17.Picture
Image1(9).Picture = Image17.Picture
End If
If black(2, 3) = True And black(3, 3) = True And white(4, 3) = True Then

Image1(8).Picture = Image17.Picture
Image1(9).Picture = Image17.Picture
Image1(10).Picture = Image17.Picture
End If
```

```vb
'check column

If black(1, 2) = True And white(1, 1) = True Then

Image1(4).Picture = Image17.Picture

Image1(8).Picture = Image17.Picture

End If

'check diagonal

If black(2, 2) = True And white(3, 1) = True Then

Image1(5).Picture = Image17.Picture

Image1(8).Picture = Image17.Picture

End If

Case "black"

If white(2, 3) = True And black(3, 3) = True Then

Image1(8).Picture = Image18.Picture

Image1(9).Picture = Image18.Picture

End If

If white(2, 3) = True And white(3, 3) = True And black(4, 2) = True Then

Image1(8).Picture = Image18.Picture

Image1(9).Picture = Image18.Picture

Image1(10).Picture = Image18.Picture

End If

If white(1, 2) = True And black(1, 1) = True Then

Image1(4).Picture = Image18.Picture

Image1(8).Picture = Image18.Picture

End If
```

56

```
If white(2, 2) = True And black(3, 1) = True Then

Image1(5).Picture = Image18.Picture

Image1(8).Picture = Image18.Picture

End If

End Select

End If

'To compute position (4,3)

If Index = 11 And black(4, 3) = False And white(4, 3) = False Then

Select Case imgtag

Case "white"

'Check Left

If black(3, 3) = True And white(2, 3) = True Then

Image1(10).Picture = Image17.Picture

Image1(11).Picture = Image17.Picture

End If

If black(3, 3) = True And black(2, 3) = True And white(1, 3) = True Then

Image1(9).Picture = Image17.Picture

Image1(10).Picture = Image17.Picture

Image1(11).Picture = Image17.Picture

End If

'check column

If black(4, 2) = True And white(4, 1) = True Then

Image1(7).Picture = Image17.Picture

Image1(11).Picture = Image17.Picture

End If
```

```vb
'check diagonal
If black(3, 2) = True And white(2, 1) = True Then
Image1(6).Picture = Image17.Picture
Image1(11).Picture = Image17.Picture
End If

Case "black"
If white(3, 3) = True And black(2, 3) = True Then
Image1(10).Picture = Image18.Picture
Image1(11).Picture = Image18.Picture
End If
If white(3, 3) = True And white(2, 3) = True And black(1, 3) = True Then
Image1(9).Picture = Image18.Picture
Image1(10).Picture = Image18.Picture
Image1(11).Picture = Image18.Picture
End If
If white(4, 2) = True And black(4, 1) = True Then
Image1(7).Picture = Image18.Picture
Image1(11).Picture = Image18.Picture
End If
If white(3, 2) = True And black(2, 1) = True Then
Image1(6).Picture = Image18.Picture
Image1(11).Picture = Image18.Picture
End If
End Select
End If
```

```vb
'To compute position (1,4)

If Index = 12 And black(1, 4) = False And white(1, 4) = False Then

Select Case imgtag

Case "white"

'Check row

If black(2, 4) = True And white(3, 4) = True Then

Image1(12).Picture = Image17.Picture

Image1(13).Picture = Image17.Picture

End If

If black(2, 4) = True And black(3, 4) = True And white(4, 4) = True Then

Image1(12).Picture = Image17.Picture

Image1(13).Picture = Image17.Picture

Image1(14).Picture = Image17.Picture

End If

'check column

If black(1, 3) = True And white(1, 2) = True Then

Image1(8).Picture = Image17.Picture

Image1(12).Picture = Image17.Picture

End If

If black(1, 3) = True And black(1, 2) = True And white(1, 1) = True Then

Image1(4).Picture = Image17.Picture

Image1(8).Picture = Image17.Picture

Image1(12).Picture = Image17.Picture

End If
```

59

```
'check diagonal
If black(2, 3) = True And white(3, 2) = True Then
Image1(9).Picture = Image17.Picture
Image1(12).Picture = Image17.Picture
End If

If black(2, 3) = True And black(3, 2) = True And white(4, 1) = True Then
Image1(6).Picture = Image17.Picture
Image1(9).Picture = Image17.Picture
Image1(12).Picture = Image17.Picture
End If
Case "black"
'Check row
If white(2, 4) = True And black(3, 4) = True Then
Image1(12).Picture = Image18.Picture
Image1(13).Picture = Image18.Picture
End If

If white(2, 4) = True And white(3, 4) = True And black(4, 4) = True Then
Image1(12).Picture = Image18.Picture
Image1(13).Picture = Image18.Picture
Image1(14).Picture = Image18.Picture
End If
'check column
If white(1, 3) = True And black(1, 2) = True Then
Image1(4).Picture = Image18.Picture
Image1(8).Picture = Image18.Picture
```

```vb
End If

If white(1, 3) = True And black(1, 2) = True And black(1, 1) = True Then

Image1(4).Picture = Image18.Picture

Image1(8).Picture = Image18.Picture

Image1(12).Picture = Image18.Picture

End If

'check diagonal

If white(2, 3) = True And black(3, 2) = True Then

Image1(9).Picture = Image18.Picture

Image1(12).Picture = Image18.Picture

End If

If white(2, 3) = True And white(3, 2) = True And black(4, 1) = True Then

Image1(6).Picture = Image18.Picture

Image1(9).Picture = Image18.Picture

Image1(12).Picture = Image18.Picture

End If

End Select

End If

'To compute position (2,4)

If Index = 13 And black(2, 4) = False And white(2, 4) = False Then

Select Case imgtag

Case "white"

'Check row

If black(3, 4) = True And white(4, 4) = True Then

Image1(13).Picture = Image17.Picture
```

```vb
Image1(14).Picture = Image17.Picture
End If

'check column

If black(2, 3) = True And white(2, 2) = True Then
Image1(9).Picture = Image17.Picture
Image1(13).Picture = Image17.Picture
End If
If black(2, 3) = True And black(2, 2) = True And white(2, 1) = True Then
Image1(5).Picture = Image17.Picture
Image1(9).Picture = Image17.Picture
Image1(13).Picture = Image17.Picture
End If

'check diagonal

If black(3, 3) = True And white(4, 2) = True Then
Image1(10).Picture = Image17.Picture
Image1(13).Picture = Image17.Picture
End If
Case "black"
'Check row
If white(3, 4) = True And black(4, 4) = True Then
Image1(13).Picture = Image18.Picture
Image1(14).Picture = Image18.Picture
End If

'check column

If white(2, 3) = True And black(2, 2) = True Then
```

```vb
Image1(9).Picture = Image18.Picture

Image1(13).Picture = Image18.Picture

End If

If white(2, 3) = True And white(2, 2) = True And black(2, 1) = True Then

Image1(5).Picture = Image18.Picture

Image1(9).Picture = Image18.Picture

Image1(13).Picture = Image18.Picture

End If

'check diagonal

If white(3, 3) = True And black(4, 2) = True Then

Image1(10).Picture = Image18.Picture

Image1(13).Picture = Image18.Picture

End If

End Select

End If

'To compute position (3,4)

If Index = 14 And black(3, 4) = False And white(3, 4) = False Then

Select Case imgtag

Case "white"

'Check row

If black(2, 4) = True And white(1, 4) = True Then

Image1(13).Picture = Image17.Picture

Image1(14).Picture = Image17.Picture

End If
```

63

```
'check column

If black(3, 3) = True And white(3, 2) = True Then

Image1(10).Picture = Image17.Picture

Image1(14).Picture = Image17.Picture

End If

If black(3, 3) = True And black(3, 2) = True And white(3, 1) = True Then

Image1(6).Picture = Image17.Picture

Image1(10).Picture = Image17.Picture

Image1(14).Picture = Image17.Picture

End If

'check diagonal

If black(2, 3) = True And white(1, 2) = True Then

Image1(9).Picture = Image17.Picture

Image1(14).Picture = Image17.Picture

End If

Case "black"

'Check row

If white(2, 4) = True And black(1, 4) = True Then

Image1(13).Picture = Image18.Picture

Image1(14).Picture = Image18.Picture

End If

'check column

If white(3, 3) = True And black(3, 2) = True Then

Image1(10).Picture = Image18.Picture

Image1(14).Picture = Image18.Picture
```

End If

If white(3, 3) = True And white(3, 2) = True And black(3, 1) = True Then

Image1(6).Picture = Image18.Picture

Image1(10).Picture = Image18.Picture

Image1(14).Picture = Image18.Picture

End If

'check diagonal

If white(2, 3) = True And black(1, 2) = True Then

Image1(9).Picture = Image18.Picture

Image1(14).Picture = Image18.Picture

End If

End Select

End If

'To compute position (4,4)

If Index = 15 And black(4, 4) = False And white(4, 4) = False Then

Select Case imgtag

Case "white"

'Check row

If black(3, 4) = True And white(2, 4) = True Then

Image1(14).Picture = Image17.Picture

Image1(15).Picture = Image17.Picture

End If

If black(3, 4) = True And black(2, 4) = True And white(1, 4) = True Then

Image1(13).Picture = Image17.Picture

Image1(14).Picture = Image17.Picture

```
Image1(15).Picture = Image17.Picture
End If
'check column
If black(4, 3) = True And white(4, 2) = True Then
Image1(11).Picture = Image17.Picture
Image1(15).Picture = Image17.Picture
End If

If black(4, 3) = True And black(4, 2) = True And white(4, 1) = True Then
Image1(7).Picture = Image17.Picture
Image1(11).Picture = Image17.Picture
Image1(15).Picture = Image17.Picture
End If

'check diagonal
If black(3, 3) = True And white(2, 2) = True Then
Image1(10).Picture = Image17.Picture
Image1(15).Picture = Image17.Picture
End If

If black(3, 3) = True And black(2, 2) = True And white(1, 1) = True Then
Image1(5).Picture = Image17.Picture
Image1(10).Picture = Image17.Picture
Image1(15).Picture = Image17.Picture
End If

Case "black"
'Check row
```

```
If white(3, 4) = True And black(2, 4) = True Then
Image1(14).Picture = Image18.Picture
Image1(15).Picture = Image18.Picture
End If

If white(3, 4) = True And white(2, 4) = True And black(1, 4) = True Then
Image1(13).Picture = Image18.Picture
Image1(14).Picture = Image18.Picture
Image1(15).Picture = Image18.Picture
End If

'check column
If white(4, 3) = True And black(4, 2) = True Then
Image1(11).Picture = Image18.Picture
Image1(15).Picture = Image18.Picture
End If

If white(4, 3) = True And white(4, 2) = True And black(4, 1) = True Then
Image1(7).Picture = Image18.Picture
Image1(11).Picture = Image18.Picture
Image1(15).Picture = Image18.Picture
End If

'check diagonal
If white(3, 3) = True And black(2, 2) = True Then
Image1(10).Picture = Image18.Picture
Image1(15).Picture = Image18.Picture
End If
```

```
If white(3, 3) = True And white(2, 2) = True And black(1, 1) = True Then
Image1(5).Picture = Image18.Picture
Image1(10).Picture = Image18.Picture
Image1(15).Picture = Image18.Picture
End If
End Select
End If
countcolor
If w + b = 16 Or b = 0 Or w = 0 Then
If w > b Then
Label5.Visible = True
Label5.Caption = " White Wins"
Else
Label5.Visible = True
Label5.Caption = "Black Wins"
End If
End If
End Sub
Sub checkstatus()
k = 0
For j = 1 To 4
For i = 1 To 4
If Image1(k).Picture = Image17.Picture Then
  white(i, j) = True
  Else: white(i, j) = False
End If
```

```
If Image1(k).Picture = Image18.Picture Then
    black(i, j) = True
Else
black(i, j) = False
  End If
k = k + 1
Next i
Next j
End Sub
Sub countcolor()
k = 0
w = 0
b = 0
For j = 1 To 4
For i = 1 To 4

If Image1(k).Picture = Image17.Picture Then
  white(i, j) = True
  w = w + 1
    Else: white(i, j) = False
End If

If Image1(k).Picture = Image18.Picture Then
    black(i, j) = True
    b = b + 1
Else
black(i, j) = False
```

```
    End If
k = k + 1
Print n
Next i
Next j
Label3.Caption = Str$(w)
Label4.Caption = Str$(b)
End Sub
```

1.9 Snakes and Ladders Game

Snakes and Ladders game is a popular board game for young children. This game usually involves two or more players who take turns to move by rolling a die. On the way to the finishing point, the players will encounter several obstacles in the form of snakes and some opportunities in the form of ladders. Whenever the player encounters a snake, or more accurately, the snake's head, he or she will be thrown back to an earlier position, which is at the snake's tail. On the other hand, whenever the player encounters a ladder, he or she can climb up the ladder to a higher position. The player who reaches the finishing point first wins the game. The UI is as shown in Figure 1.10.

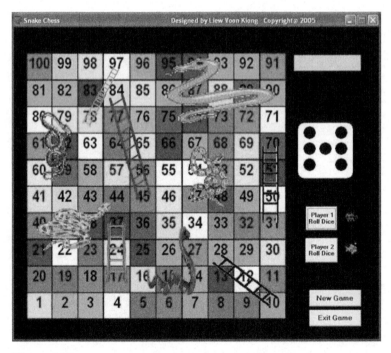

Figure 1.10

To design the program, we must apply some mathematical logics. Since the board comprises 10 rows and 10 columns, each box thus represents a cell with the relevant coordinates (column, row). Therefore, you need to define the coordinates of every cell by declaring two arrays, row (10) and col (10) respectively at the beginning of the procedure. To move the piece on the board, you can use the method **object.move** col(i), row(j), where the program can initiate the values of col(i) and row(j) via a For...Next loop. As the motion is in a zigzag manner, you must control the motion using reverse order and by imposing some conditions.

The first step in creating the game is to design the board using 100 Label controls. The Label controls are numbered from 1 to 100. You shall fill these labels with different colors to give it a more appealing look. Next, insert several pictures of snakes using the image box and then draw the ladders using the line tool. In addition, you need to draw the die with the shape control, and add in the command buttons for rolling the die, starting a new game as well as exiting the game. Besides that, you need to insert two images to denote the players and then insert a Label for the declaration of the winner. Lastly, insert two timers for animation purpose.

The initial part of the program is to declare various variables. The two most important variables are the arrays c (10) and r (10). The array r (10) represents row numbers, where r(1)=row 1, r(2)=row 2 until r(10)=row 10. Similarly, c (10) represents the column numbers, where c (1) =column 1, c (2) =column 2 until c (10) =column 10. After declaring the variables, you need to assign the coordinates of the center of all the boxes which is denoted by (column, row) or (c (i), r (i)), using the procedure below:

```
Private Sub Form_Load ()

c (1) = 600

r(1) = 8200

For i = 1 To 9

c (i + 1) = c (i) + 800

Next
```

```
For j = 1 To 9
r (j + 1) = r (j) - 800
Next
End Sub
```

Next, you must assign the initial position of the center of the first box (Label) by looking at its distance from the left as well as from the top, and also its width, in the properties window. In this program, the distance of the first box from the left is 400 twips, and its width is 800 twips, therefore its center is 600 twips from the left. Using the statement $c(i + 1) = c(i) + 800$ within a For…Next loop, the distance between successive columns will be fixed at 800 twips.

Similarly, the distance between rows can be determined using the same logic. The next most important step is to control the movement of the players' pieces. To do this, you must use the variables totalnum and totalnum1 to denote the accumulated scores of the die for player 1 and player 2, respectively. For example, if the first score of the die is 3 and the second score of the die is 6 for player 1, then totalnum=9. You need to write the procedure for every row individually so that motion will be in a zigzag manner as shown in Table 1.2

Table 1.2 Movement of the pieces

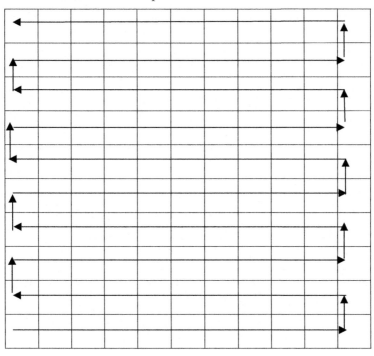

For the first row and for player 1, you can use the following procedure:

If player = 1 Then

totalnum = totalnum + num

If totalnum < 11 Then

Image1 (0).Move c (totalnum), r (1)

End If

Num is the score which appears on the die and totalnum is added to num to get the accumulated scores. In the first row, the number on the rightmost square is 10, which is equal to the number of columns across the first row. The statement Image1 (0).Move c (totalnum), r (1) uses the Move method to move piece 1 (Image1(0)) across the column from left to right . For the movement in the second row, the direction is from right to left, so you need to use the following procedure:

If totalnum > 10 And totalnum < 21 Then

Image1 (0).Move c (21 - totalnum), r (2)

End If

The statement Image1 (0).Move c(21 - totalnum), r(2) will move Image1(0) from the position c(10), r(2) to c(1), r(2), i.e. from the square with number 11 to the square with number 20. The movement of the pieces for other positions follows the same logics. The procedure to move the pieces has to be placed under the Private Sub Timer1_Timer procedure (set the Timer1's interval to a certain value).

Before the program can work, you will need to write code for the die, which will determine how many steps the pieces will move. The interface of the die consists of 7 round shapes that are placed in a rounded square as shown in Figure 1.11.

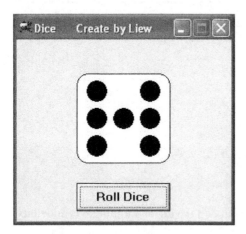

Figure 1.11

The seven round shapes are inserted as a control array with names starting with shape1 (0) to shape1 (6). The shape in the center is shape1 (3). The appearance of the round shapes are controlled by a randomization process that produce six random numbers using the statement num = Int(1 + Rnd * 6). For example, when num=1, only the round shape in the center appears while other round shapes are made invisible. Other combinations are using the same logic.

The Code

```
Option Base 1

Dim c (10) As Variant

Dim r (10) As Variant

Dim x As Integer

Dim m As Integer

Dim n As Integer

Dim num As Integer

Dim totalnum As Single

Dim totalnum1 As Single

Dim player As Integer

Dim t As Integer

 Private Sub Command2_Click()
'To move the pieces to the original position
Image1 (0).Move 10200, 5520

Image1 (1).Move 10200, 6480

Totalnum = 0

totalnum1 = 0

Label2.Caption = ""

MMControl1.Command = "close"
```

76

End Sub

Private Sub Command3_Click ()

End

End Sub

Private Sub Form_Load ()

'To assign the column and row coordinates to all the boxes

c (1) = 600

r (1) = 8200

For i = 1 To 9

c (i + 1) = c (i) + 800

Next

For j = 1 To 9

r (j + 1) = r (j) - 800

Next

End Sub

'To roll the die

Private Sub roll ()

x = x + 10

Randomize Timer

num = Int(1 + Rnd * 6)

For i = 0 To 6

   Shape1 (i).Visible = False

Next

If num = 1 Then

   Shape1 (3).Visible = True

```
   Shape2.FillColor = &HC0C0C0
 End If
If num = 2 Then
   Shape1 (2).Visible = True
   Shape1 (4).Visible = True
   Shape2.FillColor = &H8080FF
End If
If num = 3 Then
   Shape1 (2).Visible = True
   Shape1 (3).Visible = True
   Shape1 (4).Visible = True
   Shape2.FillColor = &H80FF&
 End If
If num = 4 Then
   Shape1 (0).Visible = True
   Shape1 (2).Visible = True
   Shape1 (4).Visible = True
   Shape1 (6).Visible = True
   Shape2.FillColor = &HFFFF00
 End If
If num = 5 Then
   Shape1 (0).Visible = True
   Shape1 (2).Visible = True
   Shape1 (3).Visible = True
   Shape1 (4).Visible = True
   Shape1 (6).Visible = True
```

```
    Shape2.FillColor = &HFFFF&
End If
If num = 6 Then
   Shape1 (0).Visible = True
   Shape1 (1).Visible = True
   Shape1 (2).Visible = True
   Shape1 (4).Visible = True
   Shape1 (5).Visible = True
   Shape1 (6).Visible = True
   Shape2.FillColor = &HFF00FF
 End If
End Sub

Private Sub Command1_Click (Index As Integer)
'To identify which player is clicking the roll die command
If Index = 0 Then
player = 1
End If
If Index = 1 Then
player = 2
End If
Timer1.Enabled = True
x = 0
End Sub
```

```
Private Sub Timer1_Timer ()

If x < 100 Then

Call roll

Else

Timer1.Enabled = False

'To move player 1 according to the total score of the die

'Movement across column 1 to column 10 and row 1 to row 10

If player = 1 Then

totalnum = totalnum + num

If totalnum < 11 Then

Image1 (0).Move c (totalnum), r (1)

If totalnum = 10 Then

Image1 (0).Move c (8), r (3)

totalnum = 28

End If

End If

If totalnum > 10 And totalnum < 21 Then

Image1 (0).Move c (21 - totalnum), r (2)

If totalnum = 17 Then

Image1 (0).Move c (4), r (4)

Totalnum = 37

End If

End If

If totalnum > 20 And totalnum < 31 Then
```

```
Image1 (0).Move c (totalnum - 20), r(3)

End If

If totalnum > 30 And totalnum < 41 Then

Image1 (0).Move c (41 - totalnum), r(4)

If totalnum = 34 Then

Image1 (0).Move c(5), r(2)

totalnum = 16

End If

If totalnum = 31 Then

Image1 (0).Move c (10), r (7)

totalnum = 70

End If

End If

If totalnum > 40 And totalnum < 51 Then

Image1 (0).Move c (totalnum - 40), r (5)

If totalnum = 45 Then

Image1 (0).Move c (4), r (9)

totalnum = 84

End If

If totalnum = 44 Then

Image1 (0).Move c(1), r(3)

totalnum = 21

End If

End If

If totalnum > 50 And totalnum < 61 Then

Image1 (0).Move c (61 - totalnum), r (6)
```

```
End If

If totalnum > 60 And totalnum < 71 Then

Image1 (0).Move c (totalnum - 60), r (7)

If totalnum = 68 Then

Image1 (0).Move c (8), r (5)

totalnum = 48

End If

End If

If totalnum > 70 And totalnum < 81 Then

Image1 (0).Move c (81 - totalnum), r (8)

If totalnum = 79 Then

Image1 (0).Move c (2), r (6)

totalnum = 59

End If

If totalnum = 78 Then

Image1 (0).Move c (4), r (10)

totalnum = 97

End If

End If

If totalnum > 80 And totalnum < 91 Then

Image1 (0).Move c (totalnum - 80), r (9)

End If

If totalnum > 90 And totalnum < 101 Then

Image1 (0).Move c (101 - totalnum), r (10)

If totalnum = 95 Then

Image1 (0).Move c(8), r(8)
```

```
totalnum = 73

End If

End If

If totalnum > 100 Or totalnum = 100 Then

Image1 (0).Move c (1), r(10)

End If

End If
```

'To move player 2 according to the total score of the die

```
If player = 2 Then

 totalnum1 = totalnum1 + num

If totalnum1 < 11 Then

Image1 (1).Move c (totalnum1), r(1)

If totalnum1 = 10 Then

Image1 (1).Move c (8), r(3)

totalnum1 = 28

End If

End If

If totalnum1 > 10 And totalnum1 < 21 Then

Image1 (1).Move c (21 - totalnum1), r (2)

If totalnum1 = 17 Then

Image1 (1).Move c (4), r (4)

totalnum1 = 37

End If

End If

If totalnum1 > 20 And totalnum1 < 31 Then
```

```
Image1 (1).Move c (totalnum1 - 20), r(3)

End If

If totalnum1 > 30 And totalnum1 < 41 Then

Image1 (1).Move c (41 - totalnum1), r(4)

If totalnum1 = 34 Then

Image1 (1).Move c (5), r(2)

totalnum1 = 16

End If

If totalnum1 = 31 Then

Image1(1).Move c (10), r(7)

totalnum1 = 70

End If

End If

If totalnum1 > 40 And totalnum1 < 51 Then

Image1(1).Move c(totalnum1 - 40), r(5)

If totalnum1 = 45 Then

Image1(1).Move c(4), r(9)

totalnum1 = 84

End If

If totalnum1 = 44 Then

Image1(1).Move c(1), r(3)

totalnum1 = 21

End If

End If

If totalnum1 > 50 And totalnum1 < 61 Then

Image1 (1).Move c (61 - totalnum1), r (6)
```

End If

If totalnum1 > 60 And totalnum1 < 71 Then

Image1 (1).Move c (totalnum1 - 60), r (7)

If totalnum1 = 68 Then

Image1 (1).Move c (8), r(5)

totalnum1 = 48

End If

End If

If totalnum1 > 70 And totalnum1 < 81 Then

Image1 (1).Move c (81 - totalnum1), r(8)

If totalnum1 = 79 Then

Image1 (1).Move c(2), r(6)

totalnum1 = 59

End If

If totalnum1 = 78 Then

Image1 (1).Move c (4), r (10)

totalnum1 = 97

End If

End If

If totalnum1 > 80 And totalnum1 < 91 Then

Image1 (1).Move c (totalnum1 - 80), r(9)

End If

If totalnum1 > 90 And totalnum1 < 101 Then

Image1 (1).Move c (101 - totalnum1), r (10)

If totalnum1 = 95 Then

Image1 (1).Move c (8), r (8)

```vb
totalnum1 = 73

End If

End If

If totalnum1 > 100 Or totalnum1 = 100 Then

Image1 (1).Move c (1), r (10)

End If

End If

'To play the applause sound when any one player reaches 100

If (totalnum > 100 Or totalnum = 100) And totalnum1 < 100 Then

Label2.Caption = "Player 1 Wins"

MMControl1.Notify = False

MMControl1.Wait = True

MMControl1.Shareable = False

MMControl1.DeviceType = "WaveAudio"

MMControl1.FileName = " D:\MyDocument\VB _
program\audio\applause.wav"

MMControl1.Command = "Open"

MMControl1.Command = "Play"

End If

If (totalnum1 > 100 Or totalnum1 = 100) And totalnum < 100 Then

Label2.Caption = "Player 2 Wins"

MMControl1.Notify = False

MMControl1.Wait = True

MMControl1.Shareable = False

MMControl1.DeviceType = "WaveAudio"
```

```
MMControl1.FileName = "D:\MyDocument\VB _
program\audio\applause.wav"

MMControl1.Command = "Open"

MMControl1.Command = "Play"

End If

End If

End Sub
```

1.10 Star War Game

The star war game is created using Visual Basic to demonstrate the principle of projectile, a typical physics problem. When a projectile is launched at a certain angle and with a certain initial velocity, the projectile can reach a certain range. The maximum range is at an angle of 45 degree. This principle can be applied in the military field where a missile can be launched at a specific velocity and angle to hit a remote target. It can also be applied in other scientific and technological fields. This game provides a good training for students in their abilities in making estimation. The Interface is as shown in Figure 1.12.

Figure 12

88

In this program, you can use the expression $v \sin A - \frac{1}{2}g\, t^2$ to represent the vertical component of the displacement and $v \cos A$ as the horizontal component of the displacement(where g is the gravitational acceleration , v the launch velocity and A the launch angle). To enable the missile to fly, you can use a combination of the **Object.Move** method and the object position's properties **object.left** and **Object.top**.

You also need to use randomize method so that the objects will appear at different positions randomly at each new game. In addition, you can use the randomize method to load different backgrounds at start up and at each new game.

The Code

```
Dim x As Variant

Dim a As Variant

Dim t As Variant

Dim y As Variant

Dim w As Variant

Dim i As Variant

Dim score As Integer

Dim left1, left2, left3, top1, top2, top3 As Variant

Dim backgr As Integer


Sub showfire()

Timer2.Enabled = True

End Sub

Sub reset()

'To move the missile to initial position

w = 0
```

```vb
Image1.Visible = True
Timer1.Enabled = False
Label4(0).Visible = False
Label4(1).Visible = False
Label4(2).Visible = False
Image1.Move 360, 6360
t = 0
End Sub

Private Sub Command1_Click()
Timer1.Enabled = True
End Sub

Private Sub Form_Click()
Label5.Visible = False
End Sub

Private Sub Form_Load()
left1 = Int(Rnd * 7000) + 1000
left2 = Int(Rnd * 7000) + 1000
left3 = Int(Rnd * 7000) + 1000
top1 = Int(Rnd * 5000) + 100
top2 = Int(Rnd * 5000) + 100
top3 = Int(Rnd * 5000) + 100
'To set the initial positions of the objects
Image2.Left = left1
Image3.Left = left2
Image4.Left = left3
```

```
Image2.Top = top1

Image3.Top = top2

Image4.Top = top3

w = 0

score = 0

Label7.Caption = Str$(score)

End Sub

Private Sub Image7_Click()

Label5.Visible = False

End Sub

Private Sub Instruct_Click()

Label5.Visible = True

Label5.Caption = "To play the game, you need to key in the velocity
and the angle. The range of angle should be between 0 and 90 degree.
After entering the above values, click launch to play. After every trial,
you must reset the game. After striking all the objects, press File menu
and select new game to play again."

End Sub

Private Sub mnuExit_Click()

End

End Sub

Private Sub mnunew_Click()

w = 0

Randomize Timer
```

```vb
'To display all the objects again
left1 = Int(Rnd * 7000) + 1000
left2 = Int(Rnd * 7000) + 1000
left3 = Int(Rnd * 7000) + 1000
top1 = Int(Rnd * 5000) + 100
top2 = Int(Rnd * 5000) + 100
top3 = Int(Rnd * 5000) + 100
Image2.Left = left1
Image3.Left = left2
Image4.Left = left3
Image2.Top = top1
Image3.Top = top2
Image4.Top = top3
Image2.Visible = True
Image3.Visible = True
Image4.Visible = True
Image1.Visible = True
Timer1.Enabled = False
Label4(0).Visible = False
Label4(1).Visible = False
Label4(0).Visible = False
Label3.Caption = ""
Image1.Move 360, 6360
t = 0
End Sub
```

```vb
Private Sub Timer1_Timer()

MMControl1.Command = "close"

If Image1.Left < 15000 And Image1.Top < 9000 Then

v = Val(Text1.Text)

a = Val(Text2.Text)

t = t + 1

'use the projectile formula to move the missile  y=v(sinA)t -1/2(g)sinA,
x=v(cosA)t, A=Angle of launch

y = v * Sin(a * 3.141592654 / 180) * t - 4.9 * (t ^ 2)

x = v * Cos(a * 3.141592654 / 180) * t

Image1.Move Image1.Left + x, Image1.Top - y

If Image4.Visible = True And (Image1.Left < left3 + 240 And
Image1.Left > left3 - 240) And (Image1.Top < top3 + 240 And
Image1.Top > top3 - 240) Then

i = 2

Timer1.Enabled = False

showfire

Image4.Visible = False

Image1.Visible = False

'To trigger the sound

MMControl1.Notify = False

MMControl1.Wait = True

MMControl1.Shareable = False

MMControl1.DeviceType = "WaveAudio"

MMControl1.FileName = "C:\My Documents\VB
program\audio\bomb.wav"

MMControl1.Command = "Open"
```

```
MMControl1.Command = "Play"

Label3.Caption = "You hit the satellite!"

Label4(2).Left = left3 + 240

Label4(2).Top = top3 + 240

Label4(2).Visible = True

Image5(2).Left = left3 + 240

Image5(2).Top = top3 + 240

score = score + 50

reset

ElseIf Image3.Visible = True And (Image1.Left < left2 + 240 And

Image1.Left > left2 - 240) And (Image1.Top < top2 + 240 And _

Image1.Top > top2 - 240) Then

Timer1.Enabled = False

i = 1

showfire

Image3.Visible = False

Image1.Visible = False

MMControl1.Notify = False

MMControl1.Wait = True

MMControl1.Shareable = False

MMControl1.DeviceType = "WaveAudio"

MMControl1.FileName = "C:\ My Documents\VB
program\audio\bomb.wav"

MMControl1.Command = "Open"

MMControl1.Command = "Play"

Label3.Caption = "You hit the rocket!"
```

```
Label4(1).Left = left2 + 240

Label4(1).Top = top2 + 240

Label4(1).Visible = True

Image5(1).Left = left2 + 240

Image5(1).Top = top2 + 240

score = score + 100

reset

ElseIf Image2.Visible = True And (Image1.Left < left1 + 240 And _

Image1.Left > left1 - 240) And (Image1.Top < top1 + 240 And
Image1.Top > top1 - 240) Then

Timer1.Enabled = False

i = 0

showfire

Image2.Visible = False

Image1.Visible = False

MMControl1.Notify = False

MMControl1.Wait = True

MMControl1.Shareable = False

MMControl1.DeviceType = "WaveAudio"

MMControl1.FileName = "C:\ My Documents\VB
program\audio\bomb.wav"

MMControl1.Command = "Open"

MMControl1.Command = "Play"

Label3.Caption = "You hit the Saturn!"

Label4(0).Left = left1 + 240

Label4(0).Top = top1 + 240
```

```
Label4(0).Visible = True

Image5(0).Left = left1 + 240

Image5(0).Top = top1 + 240

score = score + 200

reset

End If

Else

Label3.Caption = "You missed the target!"

Timer1.Enabled = False

reset

End If

'Show score

Label7.Caption = Str$(score)

End Sub


Private Sub Timer2_Timer()

w = w + 1

If w < 30 Then

Image5(i).Visible = True

Label4(i).Visible = True

Else

Image5(i).Visible = False

Label4(i).Visible = False

Timer2.Enabled = False

End If

End Sub
```

1.11 Tic Tac Toe

Tic Tac Toe is a popular game which you can play anytime and anywhere if you have a piece of paper and a pen, or you could draw it on sand or any surface. Now, let us program it in Visual Basic 6 so that you can play the game virtually.

To design the interface, first you need to draw four black straight lines on the form using the line control. Next, insert an image control then use copy and paste method to create nine image controls, Image1 (0) to Image1 (8) and arrange them in the following order:

Image1 (6)	Image1 (7)	Image1 (8)
Image1 (3)	Image1(4)	Image1(5)
Image1 (0)	Image1 (1)	Image1 (2)

In addition, you need to insert eight straight lines in red color that would cross out three crosses or three circles if they are aligned in a straight-line side by side, as shown in the design interface. You need to make these lines invisible at start-up and make one of the lines appear whenever the above condition is fulfilled.

Finally, insert two pictures, one in the shape of a circle and the other one is in the shape of a cross to represent player 1 and player 2 respectively. The design UI is shown in Figure 1.13

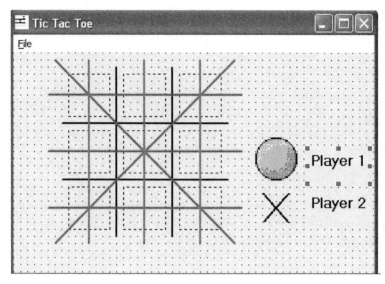

Figure 1.13

Now you need to write the code to make the game works. To check whether a position on the board is occupied or empty, you can create two arrays, **cross(8)** and **ball(8)** (you need to use ball instead of circle because circle is an internal function of VB) and declare them as Boolean. If **cross(n)=true**, it means position **n** is occupied by the player's piece which is a cross. On the other hand, **cross (n)=false** means position n is not occupied by a cross. It is the same for the **ball(n)** array. The value of n is the index of an image control. You need to create a subroutine **check_position** to check the position of the player's piece. The code is as follows:

Sub check_position()

For m = 0 To 8

If Image1(m).Picture = Image2.Picture Then

ball(m) = True

Else: ball(m) = False

End If

```
If Image1(m).Picture = Image3.Picture Then

cross(m) = True

Else

cross(m) = False

 End If

 Next

End Sub
```

Another important subroutine you need to create is **check_status** . This subroutine will check whether three similar shapes have appeared. Part of the subroutine is as follows:

```
Sub check_status()

If ball(0) = True And ball(1) = True And ball(2) = True Then

Line10.Visible = True

Player1_WinMsg

ElseIf ball(3) = True And ball(4) = True And ball(5) = True Then

Line9.Visible = True

Player1_WinMsg

ElseIf cross(0) = True And cross(1) = True And cross(2) = True Then

Line10.Visible = True

Player2_WinMsg

ElseIf cross(3) = True And cross(4) = True And cross(5) = True Then

Line9.Visible = True

Player2_WinMsg

End Sub
```

99

Both subroutines Player1_WinMsg and Player2_WinMsg are to display winning messages "Player1 win!" and "Player2 Win!" respectively.

The Code

```
Dim cross(8) As Boolean

Dim ball(8) As Boolean

Dim n, m As Integer

Dim player As Integer

'To check whether three similar images align in one straight line side by side or not

Sub check_status()

If ball(0) = True And ball(1) = True And ball(2) = True Then

Line10.Visible = True

Player1_WinMsg

ElseIf ball(3) = True And ball(4) = True And ball(5) = True Then

Line9.Visible = True

Player1_WinMsg

ElseIf ball(6) = True And ball(7) = True And ball(8) = True Then

Line8.Visible = True

Player1_WinMsg

ElseIf ball(0) = True And ball(3) = True And ball(6) = True Then

Line5.Visible = True

Player1_WinMsg

ElseIf ball(1) = True And ball(4) = True And ball(7) = True Then

Line6.Visible = True

Player1_WinMsg
```

```
ElseIf ball(2) = True And ball(5) = True And ball(8) = True Then
Line7.Visible = True
Player1_WinMsg
ElseIf ball(0) = True And ball(4) = True And ball(8) = True Then
Line12.Visible = True
Player1_WinMsg
ElseIf ball(2) = True And ball(4) = True And ball(6) = True Then
Line11.Visible = True
Player1_WinMsg
ElseIf cross(0) = True And cross(1) = True And cross(2) = True Then
Line10.Visible = True
Player2_WinMsg
ElseIf cross(3) = True And cross(4) = True And cross(5) = True Then
Line9.Visible = True
Player2_WinMsg
ElseIf cross(6) = True And cross(7) = True And cross(8) = True Then
Line8.Visible = True
Player2_WinMsg
ElseIf cross(0) = True And cross(3) = True And cross(6) = True Then
Line5.Visible = True
Player2_WinMsg
ElseIf cross(1) = True And cross(4) = True And cross(7) = True Then
Line6.Visible = True
Player2_WinMsg
ElseIf cross(2) = True And cross(5) = True And cross(8) = True Then
Line7.Visible = True
```

101

```vb
Player2_WinMsg
ElseIf cross(0) = True And cross(4) = True And cross(8) = True Then
Line12.Visible = True
Player2_WinMsg
ElseIf cross(2) = True And cross(4) = True And cross(6) = True Then
Line11.Visible = True
Player2_WinMsg
End If
End Sub

' To check the image has occupied a square or not
Sub check_position()
For m = 0 To 8
If Image1(m).Picture = Image2.Picture Then
ball(m) = True
Else: ball(m) = False
End If
If Image1(m).Picture = Image3.Picture Then
cross(m) = True
Else
cross(m) = False
End If
Next
End Sub

Private Sub Image1_Click(Index As Integer)
```

102

'To make images (cross or circle) appear on a certain position of the board

check_position

If player = 1 And cross(Index) = False And ball(Index) = False Then

Image1(Index).Picture = Image2.Picture

End If

If player = 2 And cross(Index) = False And ball(Index) = False Then

Image1(Index).Picture = Image3.Picture

End If

check_position

check_status

'To display message for a tie game (if no line visible)

n = n + 1

If n = 9 And Line5.Visible = False And _

Line6.Visible = False And Line7.Visible = False And _

Line8.Visible = False And Line9.Visible = False And _

Line10.Visible = False And Line11.Visible = False And Line12.Visible = False Then

MsgBox ("Tie!")

newgame

End If

End Sub

Private Sub Image2_Click()

player = 1

End Sub

```vb
Private Sub Image3_Click()
player = 2
End Sub

Private Sub mnuNew_Click()
newgame
End Sub

Sub Player1_WinMsg()
MsgBox ("Player1 win!")
newgame2
End Sub

Sub Player2_WinMsg()
MsgBox ("Player2 win!")
newgame2
End Sub

Sub newgame()
n = 0
For m = 0 To 8
Image1(m).Picture = LoadPicture("")
Next
Line5.Visible = False
Line6.Visible = False
Line7.Visible = False
Line8.Visible = False
Line9.Visible = False
```

104

```
Line10.Visible = False

Line11.Visible = False

Line12.Visible = False

End Sub

Sub newgame2()

n = -1

For m = 0 To 8

Image1(m).Picture = LoadPicture("")

Next

Line5.Visible = False

Line6.Visible = False

Line7.Visible = False

Line8.Visible = False

Line9.Visible = False

Line10.Visible = False

Line11.Visible = False

Line12.Visible = False

End Sub
```

The Runtime Interface is shown in Figure 1.14.

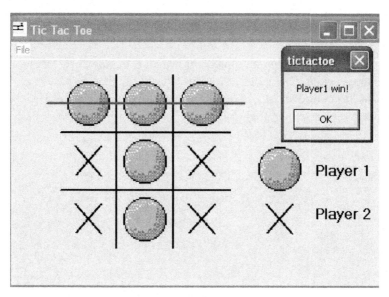

Figure 1.14

1.12 Time Bomb

This program simulates a time bomb which is ticking away and will explode within 60 seconds. To defuse the bomb, the user needs to enter the correct password otherwise the bomb will explode. The interface is shown in Figure 1.15

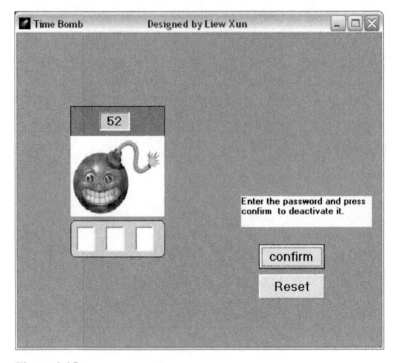

Figure 1.15

To make the program simpler, the user only needs to key-in a three-digit password which is fixed by the programmer using the declaration as follows:

    Const pw As Integer = 398

You may want to let the program creates a random password at run time using Rnd function, as follows:

```
Dim pw as Interger
pw=Int(Rnd(400))
```

To design an attractive interface, you can use the image of a bomb and an image of an exploding bomb. Make the exploding bomb image invisible at startup and make it visible only if the user fails to defuse the bomb. You also need to insert two command buttons, label one of them as **Confirm** and the other one as **Reset**. Besides, insert three text boxes to be used as the password panel. Insert a timer control and program it so that it can start the countdown. You can set the timer's interval to 1000 so that each countdown is one second, or you can set a shorter interval.

You can also insert a **Microsoft Multimedia Control** to play the explosion sound. Note that the Multimedia Control is not inlcuded in the default Toolbox; you need to add it from the component. To do that, go to the menu and click project, select components from the drop-down menu. After choosing **Microsoft Multimedia Control 6.0** from the list of available controls, the multimedia control will be added to Toolbox . To use the Microsoft Multimedia Control, drag the control into the form.

The Code

```
Private Sub Timer1_Timer ()
'To display countdown time, when it is equal to 0, it sets off the
destruction procedure

countdown = 60 - x
If countdown <= 60 And countdown > -1 Then

Lbl_Timer.Caption = Str$(countdown)
x = x + 1
ElseIf countdown < 0 Then
```

```
Timer1.Enabled = False
destruction

End If

End Sub

 MMControl1.Notify = False
MMControl1.Wait = True
MMControl1.Shareable = False
MMControl1.DeviceType = "WaveAudio"
MMControl1.FileName = "MMControl1.Notify = False"
MMControl1.Wait = True
MMControl1.Shareable = False
MMControl1.DeviceType = "WaveAudio"
MMControl1.FileName = "C:\ My Documents\VB
program\audio\bomb.wav"
MMControl1.Command = "Open"
MMControl1.Command = "Play"

End Sub
```

1.13 Lucky Draw

This is a program that simulates a lucky draw. This program consists of a 3x3 matrix comprising nine command buttons in a grid. You must define the nine command buttons as an array of controls, so that you can differentiate them by their indices. One of the buttons contains a prize, when the user clicks on it; it displays the word "**prize**" on the caption. If the user does not strike the prize, the word "**The Prize is here!**" will appear on the command button that contains the prize.

You can use a randomize process and the indices of the command buttons to create the chance events. Random integers from 1 to 9 can be created using the statement **n=Int(Rnd*9)** where **Int** is function that converts numbers to integers and **Rnd** is a method that generates random numbers between 0 and 1. When the user clicks a command button, a random number between 0 and 9 is generated and if this number corresponds to the index of the command button, it will show the word "Prize" on caption of the clicked command button , otherwise, it shows the words "The Prize is here!" on the command button with an index that corresponds to the generated number. The Interface is shown in Figure 1.16.

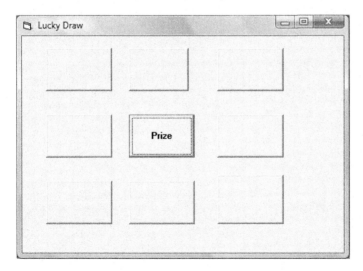

110

Figure 1.16

The Code

```
Private Sub Command1_Click(Index As Integer)
 Dim n As Integer
    For n = 0 To 8
    Command1(n).Caption = ""
    Next
    n = Int(Rnd * 9)
    If Index = n Then
    Command1(n).Caption = "Prize"
    Else: Command1(n).Caption = "The Prize is here"
    End If
End Sub
```

1.14 Boggle

Boggle is a type of words puzzle game where the players can form as many words as possible from the characters displayed on a nxn square. Words can be formed in many ways, from left to right, from right to left, top to bottom, bottom to top, diagonal, zigzag manner and more.

In this example, we have designed a 5x5 boggle. To design the Interface, insert twenty labels on the Form1. As we copy and paste each label, VB6 automatically create an array comprising Label1(0) This is only a boggle board generator, so the players must write the words on a piece of paper.

Each time we press the shake button, a different set of characters will appear. To achieve this, we use the chr() function and the Rnd function to randomly generate the characters.

Alphabet A to Z correspond to Chr(65) to chr(90), therefore we need to generate random numbers between 65 to 90. The formula to generate random numbers between two numbers is:

m = Int((MaxValue - MinValue + 1) * Rnd) + MinValue

Therefore, the formula to generate random numbers between 65 and 90 is RndNum=Int(26)+65, which means we can generate random alphabet using chr(m) in a For Next Loop.

The Code

```
Private Sub Cmd_Shake()
Dim i , m as Integer
For i = 0 To 24
        m = Int(26 * Rnd()) + 65
```

Label1(i).Caption = char(m)

Next

End Sub

The Interface is shown in Figure 1.17

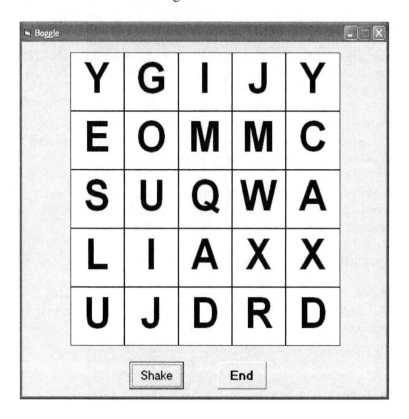

Figure 1.17

2. Educational Programs
2.1 Kid's Math

This is a simple arithmetic educational game for children. The child who attempts the test can choose three different levels and perform three different arithmetic calculations. The performance can be evaluated by three measurements namely total questions attempted, total correct answers and score which is the percentage of right answers. The Interface is shown in Figure 2.1.

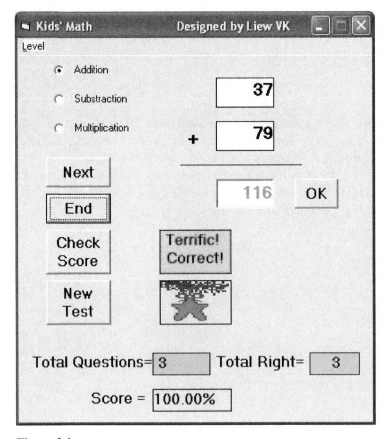

Figure 2.1

In this program, you need to add the following controls:

- Three option buttons
- Three text boxes
- A few labels
- Two images

The procedure to choose three different arithmetic calculations is

```
Private Sub Option1_Click(Index As Integer)
Select Case Index
Case 0
Label4.Caption = "+"
Action = "Plus"
Case 1
Label4.Caption = "-"
Action = "Minus"
Case 2
Label4.Caption = "x"
Action = "Multiply"
End Select
End Sub
```

The option buttons are grouped together as a control array and can be identified by their indices. Using the Select Case…End Select statements, the caption of Label4 which displays the operators will change according to the selection. In addition, the variable Action will be assigned different values namely "Plus", "Minus" and "Multiply". These values will be passed to the OK procedure and appropriate calculations will be performed.

A menu item "Level" for the user to choose the levels is added using the menu editor. To start the menu editor, you must click on the tools item on the menu bar. At the menu editor, you key in the word "Level" in the caption box and its name "level" (this can be any appropriate name) in the Name box. This is the first level menu item. To type in the second menu items, you need to click on the Next button and the right arrow key. Here you key in the words

116

Beginner, Intermediate and Advanced. The ampersand sign '&' is used in front of all the captions (it can be in any position) so that the user can use the shortcut key to access the items. For example, to access the Level item, the user can press Alt+L.

You will notice that all the menu items will appear in the code window and you can write the event procedure for each of them. The event procedure for each of the second level menu items is quite simple. It simply assigns a value to the variable n, which is n=1 for beginner, n=2 for intermediate and n=3 for advanced.

The procedure to randomize the process of displaying different numbers after each click of the command button "Start" or "Next" (The Start button changes to Next after the first Click) is shown below. The **select Case …..End Select** statements allow the generation of numbers for the three different levels.

```
Select Case n
Case 1
num1 = Int(Rnd * 10)
num2 = Int(Rnd * 10)
Case 2
num1 = Int(Rnd * 90) + 10
num2 = Int(Rnd * 90) + 10
Case 3
num1 = Int(Rnd * 900) + 100
num2 = Int(Rnd * 900) + 100
End Select
```

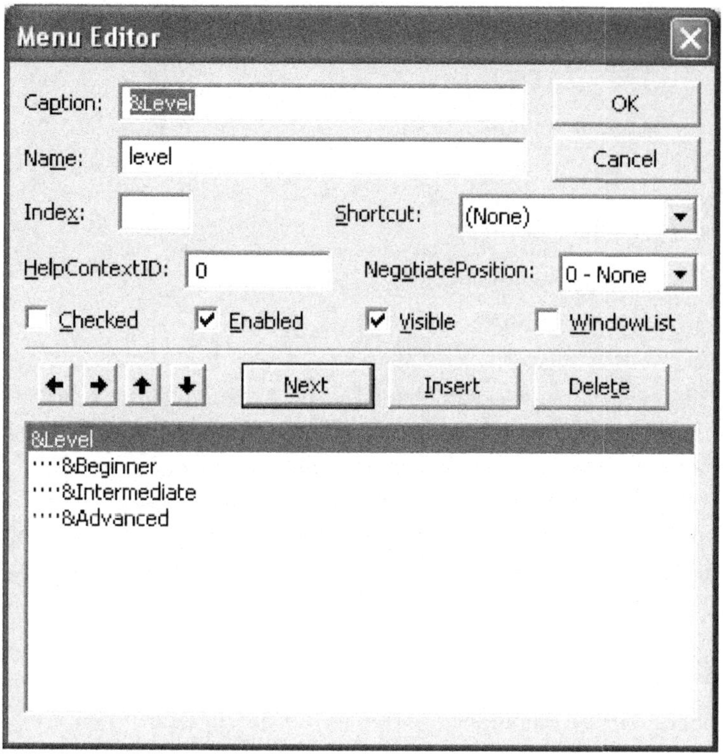

117

Figure 2.2

There are some minor things to be considered before the actual calculation is done. First, for subtraction, you need to make sure that the value of the first number is more than the second number as this is arithmetic for kids. This is taken care of using the following statement:

Case "Minus"

118

```
If num1 > num2 Then

number1.Caption = num1

number2.Caption = num2

Else

number1.Caption = num2

number2.Caption = num1

End If
```

The above statements ensure that when the second number is larger than the first number, the second number will appear in the first text box and the first number will appear in the second text box. Secondly, to make sure that the multiplication is not too complicated, the second number will be restricted to values between 0 and 10. This can be achieved using the Right function as shown in the following statements:

```
Case "Multiply"

number1.Caption = num1

number2.Caption = Right(num2, 1)
```

The actual calculation is performed under the OK procedure or the KeyPress procedure so that the user has a choice to click the OK button or press the enter key to perform the calculation. The overall program is shown below:

```
The Code

Dim num1 As Integer

Dim num2 As Integer

Dim intNumber As Integer

Dim totalQ As Integer

Dim n As Integer
```

119

```vb
Dim Action As String

Dim answer As Integer

Dim done As Boolean

Dim score As Integer

Private Sub beginner_Click()

n = 1

End Sub

Private Sub Inter_Click()

n = 2

End Sub

Private Sub advance_Click()

n = 3

End Sub


Private Sub Command3_Click ()

'To calculate the score in percentage

Label10.Caption = Format ((intNumber / totalQ), "Percent")

End Sub

Private Sub Command4_Click()

total.Caption = ""

Label8.Caption = ""

intNumber = 0

totalQ = 0

Label10.Caption = ""

Command1.Caption = "Start"
```

120

```vb
End Sub

Private Sub Form_Load()
    n=1
Option1(0).Value = True
Label4.Caption = "+"
Image1.Visible = False
Image2.Visible = False
Label6.Visible = False
Label5.Visible = False
End Sub

Private Sub Option1_Click(Index As Integer)
Select Case Index
Case 0
Label4.Caption = "+"
Action = "Plus"
Case 1
Label4.Caption = "-"
Action = "Minus"
Case 2
Label4.Caption = "x"
Action = "Multiply"
End Select
End Sub


Private Sub Text3_keypress(keyAscii As Integer)
```

```
Select Case Action
Case "Plus"
answer = Val(number1.Caption) + Val(number2.Caption)
Case "Minus"
answer = Val(number1.Caption) - Val(number2.Caption)
Case "Multiply"
answer = Val(number1.Caption) * Val(number2.Caption)
End Select
'To response to user's pressing the Enter key
If (keyAscii = 13) And answer = Val(Text3.Text) Then
Image1.Visible = True
Image2.Visible = False
Label5.Visible = True
Label6.Visible = False
If done = True Then
intNumber = intNumber + 1
total.Caption = Str(intNumber)
End If
Text3.Enabled = False
ElseIf (keyAscii = 13) And answer <> Val(Text3.Text) Then
Image1.Visible = False
Image2.Visible = True
Label5.Visible = False
Label6.Visible = True
Text3.Enabled = False
End If
```

```
End Sub

Private Sub Command1_Click()
Image1.Visible = False
Image2.Visible = False
Label6.Visible = False
Label5.Visible = False
done = True
Text3.Enabled = True
Text3.Text = ""
x = x + 1
If x > 0 Then
Command1.Caption = "Next"
End If
Randomize Timer
Select Case n
Case 1
num1 = Int(Rnd * 10)
num2 = Int(Rnd * 10)
Case 2
num1 = Int(Rnd * 90) + 10
num2 = Int(Rnd * 90) + 10
Case 3
num1 = Int(Rnd * 900) + 100
num2 = Int(Rnd * 900) + 100
End Select
```

```vb
Select Case Action
Case "Plus"
number1.Caption = num1
number2.Caption = num2
Case "Minus"
If num1 > num2 Then
number1.Caption = num1
number2.Caption = num2
Else
number1.Caption = num2
number2.Caption = num1
End If
Case "Multiply"
number1.Caption = num1
number2.Caption = Right(num2, 1)
End Select
Text3.SetFocus
totalQ = totalQ + 1
Label8.Caption = Str(totalQ)
End Sub


Private Sub OK_Click()
Select Case Action
Case "Plus"
answer = Val(number1.Caption) + Val(number2.Caption)
```

```vb
Case "Minus"
answer = Val(number1.Caption) - Val(number2.Caption)
Case "Multiply"
answer = Val(number1.Caption) * Val(number2.Caption)
End Select
If Val(Text3.Text) = answer Then
Image1.Visible = True
Image2.Visible = False
Label5.Visible = True
Label6.Visible = False
If done = True Then
intNumber = intNumber + 1
total.Caption = Str(intNumber)
End If
Else
Image1.Visible = False
Image2.Visible = True
Label5.Visible = False
Label6.Visible = True
End If
Text3.Enabled = False
done = False
End Sub
```

2.2 Pythagorean Theorem

This a program that can solve geometric problems related to Pythagorean Theorem. We supposed everybody is already familiar with the above Theorem. However, some of you may have forgotten the theorem therefore let me explain the theorem here. By referring to a right-angled triangle ABC, if the sides are AB, AC and BC respectively, where BC is the hypotenuse, then AB, AC and BC are connected by the formula   **AB²+AC²=BC²**

Using the above formula, you can calculate the third sides if the lengths of any two sides are known. For example, if AB=4 and AC=3 then BC=5. You can design the VB program for the user to input any two sides and the program is able to calculate the third side automatically. The third side BC can be found by finding the square root of AB²+AC². In visual basic, the syntax is

BC= Sqr(AB ^ 2 + AC ^ 2)

You can also use the function **Round** to let the program round the value to two decimal places using the syntax Round (BC, 2).

The Interface is shown in Figure 2.3

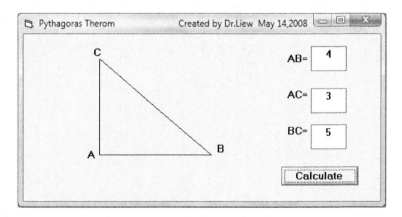

Figure 2.3

The Code

```
Private Sub Command1_Click()
Dim AB, AC, BC As Single
AB = Val(Txt_AB.Text)
AC = Val(Txt_AC.Text)
BC = Val(Txt_BC.Text)
If AB <> 0 And AC <> 0 Then
BC = Sqr(AB ^ 2 + AC ^ 2)
Txt_BC.Text = Round(BC, 2)
ElseIf AB <> 0 And BC <> 0 Then
AC = Sqr(BC ^ 2 - AB ^ 2)
Txt_AC.Text = Round(AC, 2)
ElseIf AC <> 0 And BC <> 0 Then
AB = Sqr(BC ^ 2 - AC ^ 2)
Txt_AB.Text = Round(AB, 2)
End If
End Sub
```

2.3 Factors Finder

This is a program that can find all the factors of a number entered by the user and displays them in a list box. You can use the simple logic that a number is divisible by all its factors. However, you need to tell Visual Basic how to identify factors from non-factors. To do this, you can make use of the fact that the remainder after a number is divided by its factor is zero. In Visual Basic, you can use the **MOD** operator, which compute the value of the remainder after a number is divided by an integer. The format is **N Mod x**.

With these logics in mind, you can use a **For....Next** Loop to evaluate all the remainders for all the divisors of N smaller than N. If the remainder is zero, then the divisor x (factor of x) is added to the list box.

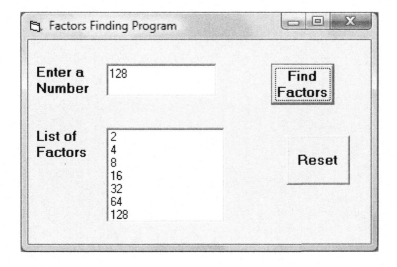

Figure 2.4

The code

```
Private Sub Command1_Click()
Dim N, x As Integer
N = Val(Text1.Text)
For x = 2 To N – 1

If N Mod x = 0 Then

List1.AddItem (x)

End If

Next

List1.AddItem (N)

End Sub
```

2.4 Prime Number Tester

This program can test whether a number is a prime number or not. A prime number is a number that cannot be divided by other numbers other than by itself. Examples are 2, 3, 5, 7, 11, 13, 17, 19, 23, 29, 31, 37 and more.

In this program, you can use the **Select Case ......End Select** statement to determine whether a number entered by a user is a prime number or not. For case 1, all numbers that are less than 2 are not prime numbers. In Case 2, if the number is 2, it is a prime number. In the final case, if the number N is more than 2, you need to divide this number by all the numbers from 3,4,5,6,.........up to N-1, if it can be divided by any of these numbers, it is not a prime number, otherwise it is a prime number. To control the program flow, you can use the **Do...Loop While** statement. Besides, you need to use **tag="Not Prime'** to identify the number that is not prime, so that when the routine exits the loop, the label will display the correct answer. The Interface is shown in Figure 2.5.

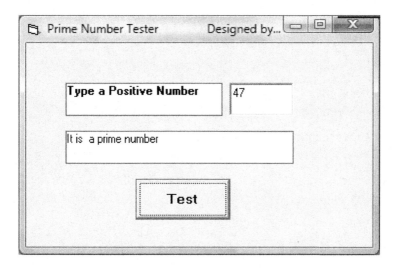

Figure 2.5

130

The Code

```
Private Sub Command1_Click()
Dim N, D  As  Single
Dim tag As String

N = Val(TxtNumber.Text)

Select Case N
Case Is < 2

Lbl_Answer.Caption = "It is not a prime number"

Case Is = 2

Lbl_Answer.Caption = "It is a prime number"

Case Is > 2
D = 2
Do
If N / D = Int(N / D) Then

Lbl_Answer.Caption = "It is not a prime number"
tag = "Not Prime"
Exit Do

End If
D = D + 1
Loop While D <= N - 1
If tag <> "Not Prime" Then

Lbl_Answer.Caption = "It is a prime number"
End If

End Select
End Sub
```

2.5 Geometric Progression

This is a program that generates a geometric progression and displays the results in a list box. Geometric progression is a sequence of numbers where each subsequent number is found by multiplying the previous number by a fixed number which is called common ratio. The common ratio can be negative, an integer, a fraction, and any number but it must not be a zero.

The general formula to find the nth term of the geometric progression is

ar^{n-1}

Where a is the first number and r is the common ratio.

In visual basic, you can employ the **Do.... Loop Until** statement to generate the numbers in a geometric progression. In this program, you need to insert three text boxes for the user to enter the first number, the common ratio, and the number of terms. You also need to insert a list box to list the numbers. Besides that, a command button is need for the user to generate the numbers in the geometric progression.

To add the numbers to the list box, use the **AddItem** method.

The syntax is **List1.AddItem** n, where n can be any variable.

The Code

```
Private Sub cmd_compute_Click()

Dim x, n, num As Integer
Dim r As Single
x = Txt_FirstNum.Text
r = Txt_CR
num = Txt_Terms.Text
```

```
List1.AddItem "n" & vbTab & "x"
List1.AddItem "_____"

n = 1
Do
x = x * r
List1.AddItem n & vbTab & x
n = n + 1
Loop Until n = num + 1

End Sub
```

The Interface

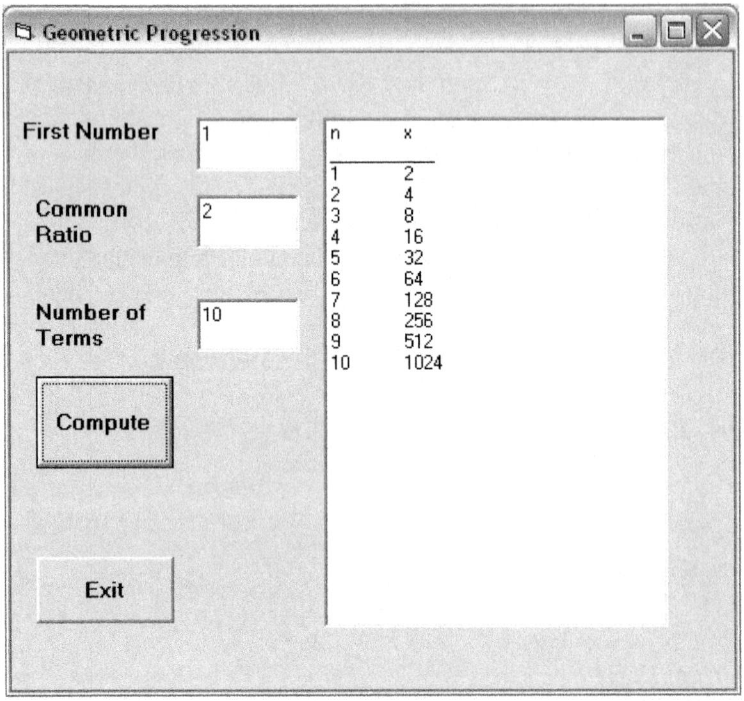

Figure 2.6

2.6 Maximum Number Calculator

This program allows the user enters three hidden numbers and it can calculate the maximum number among the three numbers. For the password user type in hidden mode, you have to set the PasswordChar property to alphanumeric symbols such as *.

Now, you can create a function called **calMax** that consists of three arguments **x, y, z**. You also need to write a procedure to call this function. This procedure employs the **If Then ElseIf** statements and the conditional operators to determine the maximum number. The function **Str** is used to convert a numeric to string.

The Code

```
Function calMax(x, y, z As Variant)

If x > y And x > z Then

calMax = Str(x)

ElseIf y > x And y > z Then

calMax = Str(y)

ElseIf z > x And z > y Then

calMax = Str(z)

End If

End Function

Private Sub Command1_Click()

Dim a, b, c
a = Val(Txt_Num1.Text)
b = Val(Txt_Num2.Text)
c = Val(Txt_Num3.Text)
Lbl_Display.Caption = calMax(a, b, c)
```

134

End Sub

The Interface is shown in Figure 2.7

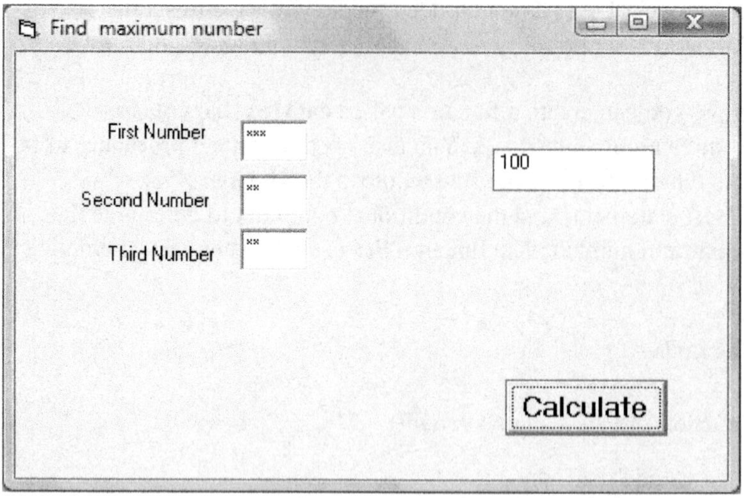

Figure 2.7

2.7 Quadratic Equation Solver

Quadratic equation is a straightforward high school mathematics problem. The quadratic equation solver was programmed to determine the number of roots the equation has as well as to compute the roots. It uses the determinant b^2 -4ac to solve the problems. If b^2 -4ac>0, then it has two roots and if b^2 -4ac=0, then it has one root, else it has no root. To obtain the roots, the program uses the standard quadratic formula as follows:

$$X = -b \pm \sqrt{\frac{b^2 - 4ac}{2a}}$$

The Code

```
Private Sub Form_Load()
Dim a, b, c, det As Integer
Dim root1, root2 As Single
Dim numroot As Integer
End Sub

Private Sub new_Click()
' To set all values to zero
Coeff_a.Text = ""
Coeff_b.Text = ""
Coeff_c.Text = ""
Answers.Caption = ""
txt_root1.Visible = False
txt_root2.Visible = False
txt_root1.Text = ""
txt_root2.Text = ""
Lbl_and.Visible = False
Lbl_numroot.Caption = ""

End Sub
```

136

```
Private Sub Solve_Click()
a = Val(Coeff_a.Text)
b = Val(Coeff_b.Text)
c = Val(Coeff_c.Text)

'To compute the value of the determinant

det = (b ^ 2) - (4 * a * c)
If det > 0 Then

Lbl_numroot.Caption = 2
root1 = (-b + Sqr(det)) / (2 * a)
root2 = (-b - Sqr(det)) / (2 * a)
Answers.Caption = "The roots are "
Lbl_and.Visible = True
txt_root1.Visible = True
txt_root2.Visible = True
txt_root1.Text = Round(root1, 4)
txt_root2.Text = Round(root2, 4)

ElseIf det = 0 Then

root1 = (-b) / 2 * a
Lbl_numroot.Caption = 1
Answers.Caption = "The root is "
txt_root1.Visible = True
txt_root1.Text = root1

Else

Lbl_numroot.Caption = 0
Answers.Caption = "There is no root "

End If
End Sub
```

The Interface is shown in Figure 2.8.

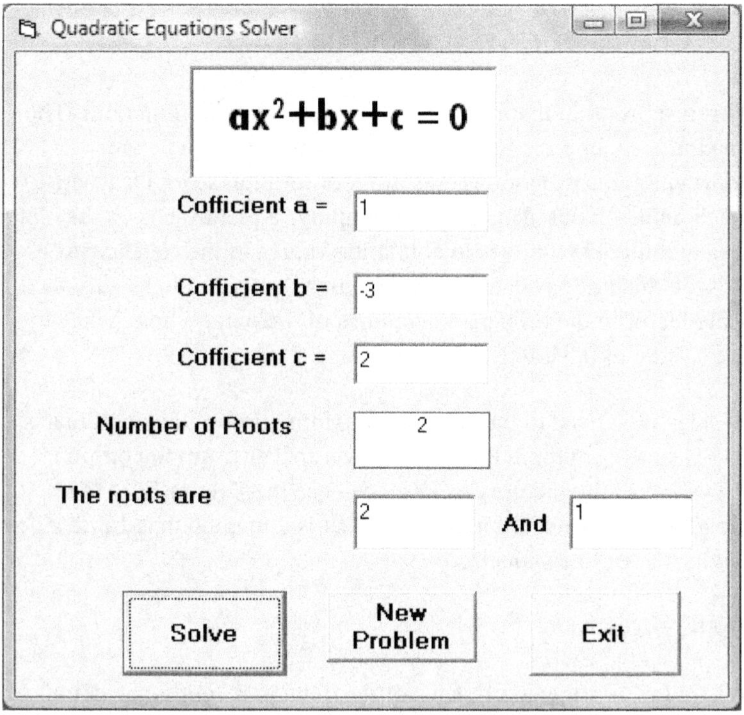
Quadratic Equations Solver
ax2+bx+c = 0
Cofficient a =
1
Cofficient b =
-3
Cofficient c =
2
Number of Roots
2
The roots are
2
And
1
Solve
New Problem
Exit

Figure 2.8

2.8 Quadratic Graph Plotter

This is a program that can plot graphs for quadratic functions. The quadratic equation is $f(x) = ax^2+bx+c$, where a, b and c are constants. This program is a useful tool for high school teachers to teach mathematics. This program employs a picture box as the plot area and three text boxes to obtain the values of the coefficients a, b, c of the quadratic equation from the user. You need to modify the scale factor in the property's windows of the picture box. You can use a scale of 0.5 cm to represent 1 unit.

Besides, you need to make some transformation as the coordinates in VB start from top left, but it is better to transform the origin to the center of the picture box. You can use the **Pset** method to draw the graph using a small increment. Pset is a method that draws a dot on the screen, the syntax is

Pset(x, y), color

Where (x, y) is the coordinates of the dot and colour is the colour of the dot. The default color is black. Using the For Next loop together with Pset, the program can draw a line on the screen.

The Code

```
Private Sub cmd_draw_Click()
Dim a, b, c As Integer
Dim w, v As Single
a = Val(txt_a.Text)
b = Val(txt_b.Text)
c = Val(txt_c.Text)
'Using a scale of 0.5 cm to represent i unit to draw the graph
For w = 0 To 10 Step 0.001
v = a * (5 - w) ^ 2 - b * (5 - w) + c
pic_graph.PSet (w, 5 - v)
Next w
End Sub
```

Private Sub Command1_Click()

pic_graph.Cls
txt_a.Text = ""
txt_b.Text = ""
txt_c.Text = ""

End Sub

The Interface is shown in Figure 2.9.

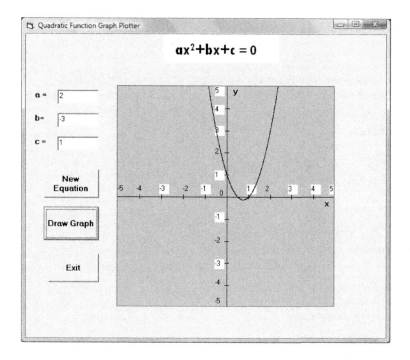

Figure 2.9

2.9 Simultaneous Equations Solvers
2.9(a) Linear Simultaneous Equations

Simultaneous equations are equations that involve two or more unknown variables. There must be as many equations as the number of unknown variables for us to solve the problem. In this example, we shall only solve linear simultaneous equations. Linear simultaneous equations take the following forms:

ax+by= m

cx+by = n

Simultaneous equations can be solved by the substitution or elimination methods. In this program, you can use the substitution method. By using the method, you can derive the following formulas:

x = (b * n - d * m) / (b * c - a * d)
y = (a * n - c * m) / (a * d - b * c)

The Code

```
Private Sub Solve_Click()
Dim a, b, c, d, m, n As Integer
Dim x, y As Double
a = Val(Txt_a.Text)
b = Val(Txt_b.Text)
m = Val(Txt_m.Text)
c = Val(Txt_c.Text)
d = Val(Txt_d.Text)
n = Val(Txt_n.Text)
x = (b * n - d * m) / (b * c - a * d)
y = (a * n - c * m) / (a * d - b * c)
Lbl_x.Caption = Round(x, 2)
Lbl_y.Caption = Round(y, 2) 'using round to limit decimal places

End Sub
```

'To get new equations
Private Sub New_Click()
Txt_a.Text = ""
Txt_b.Text = ""
Txt_m.Text = ""
Txt_c.Text = ""
Txt_d.Text = ""
Txt_n.Text = ""
Lbl_x.Caption = ""
Lbl_y.Caption = ""

End Sub

The Interface

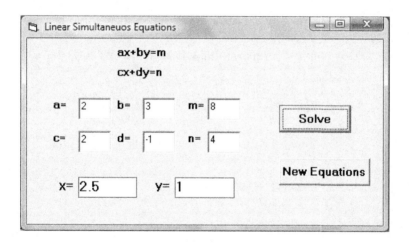

Figure 2.10

2.9(b) Mixed Simultaneous Equations

In this example, we will show you how to design a program that can solve mixed simultaneous equations, that is, one linear equation and one quadratic equation. Mixed simultaneous equations take the following forms:

ax+by=m

cx2+dy2=n

Simultaneous equations can normally be solved by the substitution or elimination methods. In this program, you can use the substitution method. So, you can obtain the following formulas:

x1 = (m a d + Sqr(m 2 a 2 d 2 - (b 2 c + a 2 d) (d m 2 - b 2 n))) / (b 2 c + a 2 d)
x2 = (m a d +-Sqr(m 2 a 2 d 2 - (b 2 c + a 2 d) (d m 2 - b 2 n))) / (b 2 c + a 2 d)

y1 = (m - a x1) / b
y2 = (m - a x2) / b

The Code

```
Private Sub Command1_Click()
Dim a, b, c, d, m, n As Integer
Dim x1, x2, y1, y2 As Double

a = Val(Txt_a.Text)
b = Val(Txt_b.Text)
m = Val(Txt_m.Text)
c = Val(Txt_c.Text)
d = Val(Txt_d.Text)
n = Val(Txt_n.Text)
x1 = (m * a * d + Sqr(m ^ 2 * a ^ 2 * d ^ 2 - (b ^ 2 * c + a ^ 2 * d) * _
```

(d * m ^ 2 - b ^ 2 * n))) / (b ^ 2 * c + a ^ 2 * d)

x2 = (m * a * d - Sqr(m ^ 2 * a ^ 2 * d ^ 2 - (b ^ 2 * c + a ^ 2 * d) *_

(d * m ^ 2 - b ^ 2 * n))) / (b ^ 2 * c + a ^ 2 * d)
y1 = (m - a * x1) / b
y2 = (m - a * x2) / b
Lbl_x1.Caption = Round(x1, 2)
Lbl_y1.Caption = Round(y1, 2)
Lbl_x2.Caption = Round(x2, 2)
Lbl_y2.Caption = Round(y2, 2)

End Sub

The Interface

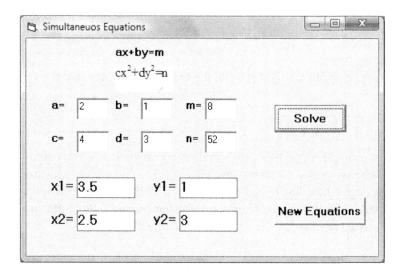

Figure 2.11

2.10. The Sine Rule

The Sine Rule can be used to calculate the remaining sides of a triangle when two angles and a side are known. It can also be used when two sides and one of the non-enclosed angles are known. In some cases, the formula may produce two possible values for the enclosed angle, leading to an ambiguous case. The sine rule is shown below.

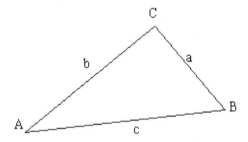

By referring to the figure above, the formula of the sine rule is:

$$\frac{a}{\sin A} = \frac{b}{\sin B} = \frac{c}{\sin C}$$

For example, if the user enters angle A and angle B as 60 and 30 respectively, and the length a=4, then b=6.93. You need to convert the degree to radian by multiplying the angle by π (=3.14159) and divide it by 180. To get more accurate value of π using the formula π=4Atn (1) where Atn is Arctangent, as Tan(π/4) =1.

The Code

```
Private Sub Cmd_Cal_Click()

Dim A, B, X, Y, m, I As Single

Dim Pi As Single

Pi = 4 * Atn(1)

A = Val(TextA.Text)

B = Val(TextB.Text)

m = Val(Text_SideA.Text)

'To convert the angle to radian

X = (Pi / 180) * A
Y = (Pi / 180) * B

I = (m * Sin(Y)) / Sin(X)

'To correct the answer to two decimal places

Lbl_Answer.Caption = Str(Format(I, "0.00"))


End Sub
```

The Interface

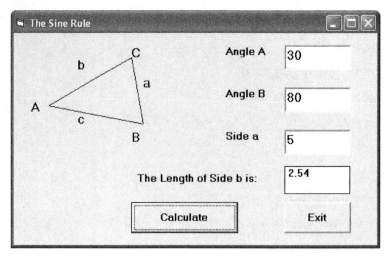

Figure 2.12

2.11 Projectile

This is a program that can plot the path of a projectile, a basic concept of missile launching. This path is determined by the launching angle and speed. The formula is **y=(Vsin a) t- 1/2(gt2)** and **x=(Vcosa)t**, where **V=launching speed** and a is the launching angle, g is acceleration due to gravity(9.8 ms-2) while t is the flight time.

In this program, you can use a picture box for drawing the parabolic curve. The command Pset is used to plot the curve. Pset is a method that draws a point on the screen. Using a looping procedure like the Do ... Loop will connect all the points into a line.

The Code

```
Private Sub cmd_Draw_Click()

Dim x, y, v, t, a As Single
v = Txt_Speed.Text
a = Txt_Angle.Text
Pic_Curve.Cls

Do
t = t + 0.01
y = v * Sin(a * 3.141592654 / 180) * t - 4.9 * (t ^ 2)
x = v * Cos(a * 3.141592654 / 180) * t
Pic_Curve.PSet (x, 120 - y)
If x > 120 Then

Exit Do

End If
Loop

End Sub
```

The Interface

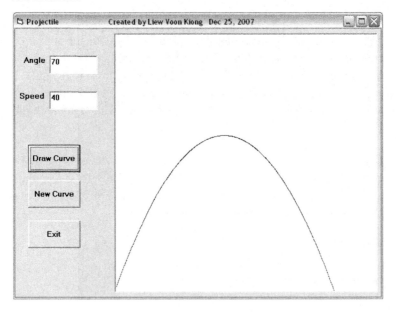

Figure 2.13

2.12 Simple Harmonic Motion

Simple harmonic motion is the motion of a simple harmonic oscillator. The motion is periodic, as it repeats itself at standard intervals in a specific manner with constant amplitude. It is characterized by its amplitude, its period which is the time for a single oscillation, its frequency which is the number of cycles per unit time, and its phase, which determines the starting point on the sine wave. The period, and its inverse the frequency, are constants determined by the overall system, while the amplitude and phase are determined by the initial conditions (position and velocity) of that system. (Wikipedia, 2008). The general equation describing simple harmonic motion is

x=Acos(2pft+f), where x is the displacement, A is the amplitude of oscillation, f is the frequency, t is the elapsed time, and f is the phase of oscillation.

To create a simple model of simple harmonic motion in Visual Basic, you can use the equation **x=Acos(wt),** and assign a value of 500 to A and a value of 50 to w. In this program, the circular object which has been inserted into the form will oscillate from left to right, reaching the maximum speed at the middle of the path.

In this program, you have to insert a shape and set it to be a circle in the properties windows. Next, insert two command buttons and change the captions to Start and Stop, respectively. Finally, insert a timer and set its interval to be 100 and disabled it at start up. You can use the move method to move the shape1 object whose path is determined by the formula **x = 500 * Cos (50 * t).** When you run the program, the object will move in an oscillating motion as shown in Figure 2.14

The Code

Dim t As Integer

Private Sub cmd_Start_Click()

Timer1.Enabled = True

End Sub

Private Sub cmd_Stop_Click()

Timer1.Enabled = False
End Sub

Private Sub Timer1_Timer()

t = t + 1
x = 500 * Cos(50 * t)
Shape1.Move Shape1.Left + x

End Sub

The Interface is shown in Figure 2.14

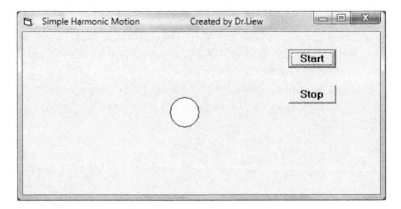

Figure 2.14

3. Financial Programs

3.1 Amortization Calculator

Before we delve into the program code, you need to know some basic financial concepts. The term loan amortization means the computation of the amount of equal periodic payments necessary to provide lender with a specific interest return and repay the loan principal over a specified period. The loan amortization process involves finding the future payments whose present value at the loan interest rate equal the amount of initial principal borrowed. Lenders use a loan amortization schedule to determine these payment amounts and the allocation of each payment to interest and principal.

The formula to calculate periodic payment is

Payment=Initial Principal/PVIFAn

PVIFAn is known as present value interest factor for an annuity. The formula to compute **PVIFAn** is

PVIFAn =1/i - 1/i(1+i)n

Where n is the number of payments. Usually you can check up a financial table for the value of PVIFAn and then calculate the payments manually. You can also use a financial calculator to compute the values. However, if you already know how to write program in VB, why not create your very own financial calculator.

To calculate the payments for interest, you can multiply the initial principal with the interest rate, and then use periodic payment to minus payment for interest. To calculate the balance at the end of a period, you can use the formula

End-of-year principal=Beginning-of-year principal - periodic payment

In this program, you need to add four text boxes to accept the input for initial principal value, number of payments, interest rate per annum and amount of periodic payments. You also need to insert a list box to display the amortization table.

The Code

```
Dim Num, n As Integer
Dim I, P, PVIFA, r, pmt, PI, PP As Double

Public Sub Cmd_Calculate_Click()

P = Txt_Principal.Text
Num = Txt_Num_payment.Text
r = Txt_Interest.Text
I = r / 100
PVIFA = 1 / I - 1 / (I * (1 + I) ^ Num)
pmt = P / PVIFA
Lbl_Amtpayment.Caption = Round(pmt, 2)

End Sub

Private Sub Cmd_Create_Click()

List_Amortization.AddItem "n" & vbTab & "Periodic" & vbTab & vbTab
& "Payment" & vbTab & vbTab & "Payment" & vbTab & vbTab &
"Balance"
List_Amortization.AddItem "" & vbTab & "Payment" & vbTab & vbTab
& "Interest" & vbTab & vbTab & "Principal"
List_Amortization.AddItem
"_____"
Do
n = n + 1
PI = P * I
PP = pmt - PI
P = P - PP
List_Amortization.AddItem n & vbTab & Round(pmt, 2) & vbTab &
vbTab & Round(PI, 2) & vbTab & vbTab & Round(PP, 2) & vbTab &
```

153

```
vbTab & Round(P, 2)
If n = Num Then
Exit Do
End If

Loop

End Sub
```

The Interface is shown in Figure 3.1.

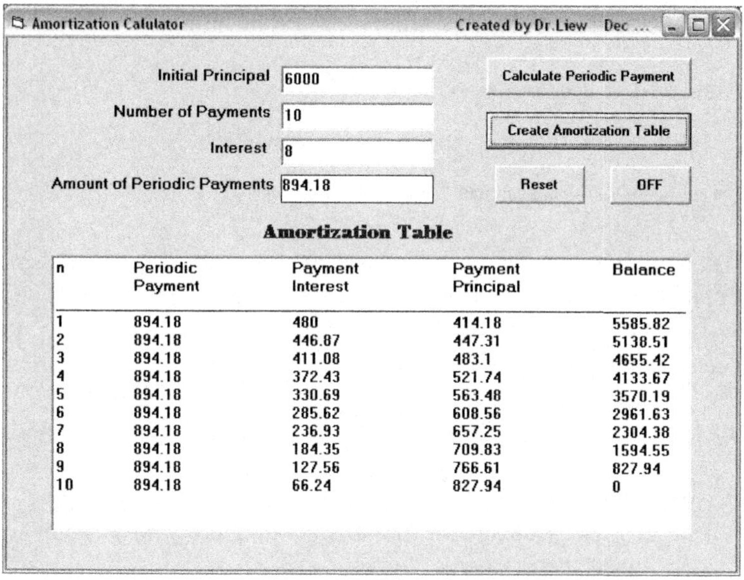

Figure 3.1

3.2 Depreciation Calculator

Depreciation means a reduction in the value of an asset with the passage of time. Depreciation is computed based on the initial purchase price or initial cost, number of years where depreciation is calculated, salvage value at the end of the depreciation period, and the asset's life span.

Depreciation is an important element in the management of a company's assets. With proper and accurate calculation of depreciation, a company can benefit from the tax advantage. In Visual Basic, the syntax of the depreciation function is

DDB(Cost,Salvage,Life, Period)

Cost=Initial cost, Salvage=Salvage value, Life=Asset's life span

Period=Depreciation period

In this program, you need to add four text boxes to accept input for initial cost, salvage value, asset's life, and period of depreciation. Besides that, insert a label to display the amount of depreciation and a command button to compute the depreciation.

The Code

```
Private Sub Command1_Click()

Dim Int_Cost, Sal_Value, Asset_Life, Deperiod, Depre_Amt As Double
Int_Cost = Val(Txt_Cost.Text)
Sal_Value = Val(Txt_Salvage.Text)
Asset_Life = Val(Txt_Life.Text)
Deperiod = Val(Txt_Period.Text)
Depre_Amt = DDB(Int_Cost, Sal_Value, Asset_Life, Deperiod)
Lbl_Dpre.Caption = Format(Depre_Amt, "$###,###,000.00")
End Sub
```

The Interface shown in Figure 3.2

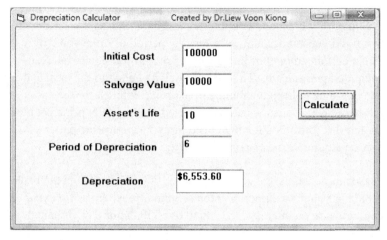

Figure 3.2

3.3 Future Value Calculator

The concept of future value is related to time value of money. For example, if you deposit your money in a bank as a savings account or a fixed deposit account for a specific period of time, you will earn a certain amount of interest based on the compound interest computed periodically. This amount will be added to the principal if you continue to keep the money in the bank. Interest for the following period is now computed based on the initial principal plus the interest (the amount which becomes your new principal). Subsequent interests are computed in the same way.

For example, let us say you deposited $1000 in a bank and the bank is paying you 5% compound interest annually. After the first year, you will earn an interest of $1000x0.05=$50. Your new principal will be

$1000+$1000x0.05=$1000(1+0.05) =$1000(1.05) =$1050.

After the second year, your new principal will be

$1000(1.05) x1.05=$1000(1.05)2 =$1102.50.

This new principal is called the future value.

Following the above calculation, the future value after n years will be

$$FV = PV * (1 + i / 100)^n$$

Where PV represents the present value, FV represents the future value, is the interest rate and n is the number of periods (Normally months or years).

The code

```
Public Function FV(PV As Variant, i As Variant, n As Variant) As Variant
'Formula to calculate Future Value(FV)
'PV denotes Present Value
FV = PV * (1 + i / 100) ^ n

End Function
Private Sub compute_Click()

'This procedure will calculate Future Value
Dim FutureVal As Currency
Dim PresentVal As Currency
Dim interest As Variant
Dim period As Variant
PresentVal = PV.Text
interest = rate.Text
period = years.Text
FutureVal = FV(PresentVal, interest, period)
Label5.Caption = Format(FutureVal, "currency")
End Sub
```

The Interface is shown in Figure 3.3

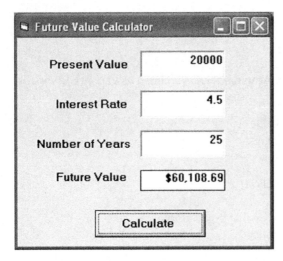

Figure 3.3

3.4 Investments Calculator

This program is basically the same as the Future Value Calculator in the previous section, where you can use the formula $FV = PV * (1 + i / 100)$ n to calculate the future value. However, in this example, we assume you have a target future value in mind, and you wish to know how much money you need to invest to achieve the target based on a certain interest. Though you still can employ the same basic formula, this time you can use the Visual Basic 6 built-in present value function, or PV.

The syntax of the PV function is

PV(Rate,Nper, Pmt,FV,Due)

Rate=Interest rate, Nper=The length of period (Usually number of years)

Pmt=Periodic payment, FV=Future Value

*Due= 1 if payment due at beginning of a period and Due=0 if payment due at the end of a period. In our example, you can consider a single initial investment in order to earn a certain amount of money in the future, so Pmt is set to 0, and payment due is at the beginning of the period, so it is set at 0, the rest of the values are obtained from the users.

The Code

```
Private Sub cmdCal_Click()

Dim F_Money, Int_Rate, Investment As Double
Dim numYear As Single
F_Money = Val(Txt_FV.Text)
Int_Rate = (Val(Txt_Rate.Text) / 100)
numYear = Val(Txt_Year.Text)
Investment = PV(Int_Rate, numYear, 0, F_Money, 1)
Lbl_PV.Caption = Format(-Investment, "$##,###,##0.00")
```

160

End Sub

The Interface is as shown in Figure 3.5

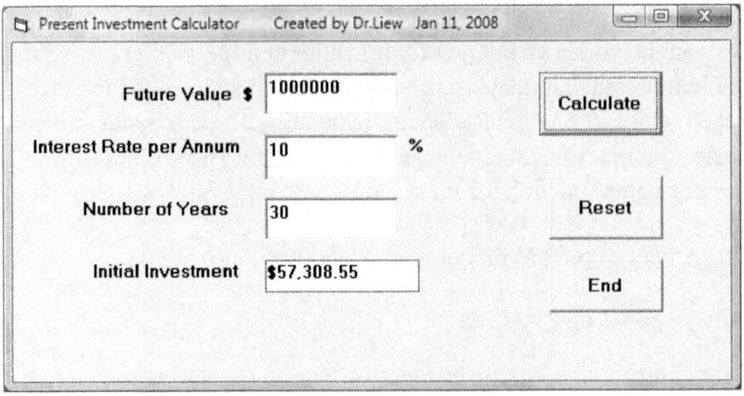

Figure 3.5

3.5 Payback Period Calculator

Currently people seem to face a lot of difficulties to secure a loan or have problem to pay back a loan. The subprime loan issues seem to hit everyone hard. Still, we need to borrow money every now and then to acquire an asset or to pay for education fees. So, naturally we need to find out how long we can settle a loan for a certain amount of monthly payment at a certain interest rate. It is not easy to calculate such figure; fortunately, Visual Basic comes to the rescue. There is built-in function in VB to calculate the payback period is Nper and the syntax is

Nper(Rate,Pmt,PV,FV,Due)

Rate=Interest Rate

Pmt=Amount of Periodic Payment

PV=Loan taken

FV=Future Value (set to 0 if loan is settled)

Due=set to 1 if payment at the beginning of the period

     set to 0 if payment at the end of the period

The Code

```
Private Sub Command1_Click()

Dim payment, Loan, Int_Rate As Double
Dim Num_year As Single
payment = Val(Txt_Payment.Text)
Int_Rate = (Val(Txt_Rate.Text) / 100) / 12
Loan = Val(Txt_PV.Text)
Num_year = NPer(Int_Rate, payment, -Loan, 0, 0) / 12
Lbl_Period.Caption = Str(Int(Num_year))

End Sub
```

The Interface is as shown in Figure 3.6

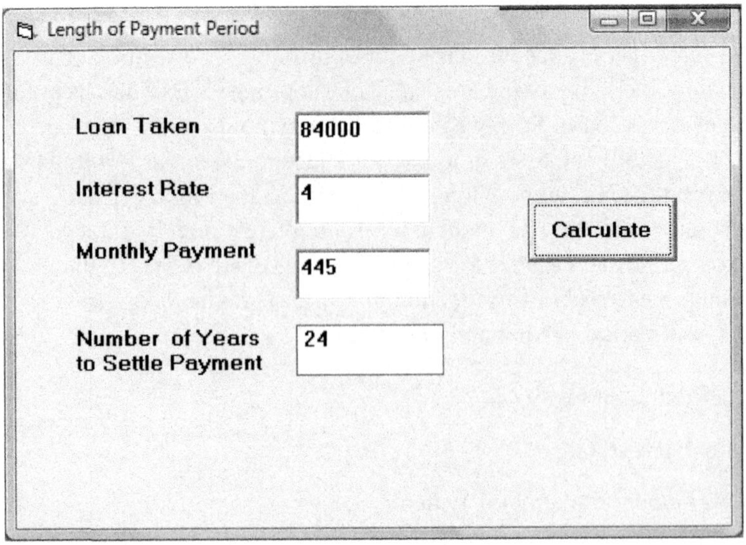

162

Length of Payment Period

Loan Taken: 84000

Interest Rate: 4

Monthly Payment: 445

Number of Years to Settle Payment: 24

Calculate

Figure 3.6

4. Graphics Programs
4.1 Drawing Pad

You can create a virtual drawing program using Visual Basic 6. You may call it drawing pad.

In this program, the user needs to fill in all the coordinates and chooses a colour before he or she can proceed to draw the required shape. If he or she forgets to fill in the coordinates or chooses a colour, he or she will be prompted to do so.

To create the drawing pad, you need to insert a common dialog control, a picture box, four text boxes, six command buttons and the necessary labels. The function of the common dialog control is to assist the users to choose colours. The text boxes are for the user to enter the coordinates and the picture box is to display the pictures drawn.

The syntax to draw a straight line is Line, and the syntax is as follows:

Picture1.Line (x1, y1)-(x2, y2), color

Where picture1 is the picture box, (x1, y1) is the coordinates of the starting point, (x2, y2) is the ending point and color understandably is the color of the line.

The syntax to draw a non-solid rectangle is

Picture1.Line (x1, y1)-(x2, y2), color, B

The syntax to draw a solid rectangle is

Picture1.Line (x1, y1)-(x2, y2), color, BF

The syntax to draw a circle is

Picture1.Circle (x3, y3), r, color

(x 3, y3) the centre of the circle, and r is the radius.

If you wish to draw a solid circle and fill it with the selected color, then add two more lines to the above syntax:

```
Picture1.FillStyle = vbSolid
Picture1.FillColor = color
```

The syntax to clear the picture is

```
Picture1.Cls
```

The code

```
Private Sub cmd_Rectangle_Click()

x1 = Text1.Text
y1 = Text2.Text
x2 = Text3.Text
y2 = Text4.Text
Picture1.Line (x1, y1)-(x2, y2), color, B

End Sub


Private Sub cmd_Color_Click()

CommonDialog1.Flags = &H1&
CommonDialog1.ShowColor
color = CommonDialog1.color

End Sub


Private Sub cmd_Circle_Click()

On Error GoTo addvalues

x3 = Text5.Text
y3 = Text6.Text
r = Text7.Text

Picture1.FillStyle = vbSolid

Picture1.FillColor = color

Picture1.Circle (x3, y3), r, color
```

165

Exit Sub

addvalues:

MsgBox ("Please fill in the coordinates ,the radius and the color")

End Sub

Private Sub Command5_Click()

Picture1.Cls

```
End Sub
Private Sub cmd_SolidRect_Click()
x1 = Text1.Text
y1 = Text2.Text
x2 = Text3.Text
y2 = Text4.Text
Picture1.Line (x1, y1)-(x2, y2), color, BF
```

End Sub

The Interface is shown in Figure 4.1

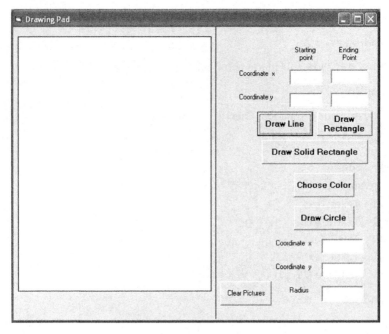

Figure 4.1

4.2 Picture Viewer

This is a program that enables the user to browse, open and chooses image files from the folders in his or her computer and views them in a picture box. There are two ways to implement the program. The first is to build the program from the ground up and the second makes use of the common dialog box.

The first way is a little more complicated, but you can learn a great deal of programming techniques. To create this program, you need to insert a drive list box (**DriveListBox**) , a directory list box (**DirListBox**), a file list box(**FileListBox**) and a combo box . The drive list box is for the user to select a drive, the directory list box is for the user to choose a folder and the file list box is display the files in the selected folder. Besides that, the combo box allows the user to select all graphics files or all files. You also need to insert a picture box to display the image.

The code for First Method

```
Private Sub Combo1_Change()
'To list all graphics files or all files
If ListIndex = 0 Then
File1.Pattern = ("*.bmp;*.wmf;*.jpg;*.gif")
Else
Fiel1.Pattern = ("*.*")
End If

End Sub
Private Sub Dir1_Change() 'To choose drive

File1.Path = Dir1.Path
File1.Pattern = ("*.bmp;*.wmf;*.jpg;*.gif")

End Sub

Private Sub Drive1_Change()
Dir1.Path = Drive1.Drive
```

168

```
End Sub

Private Sub File1_Click()
'To select a file
If Combo1.ListIndex = 0 Then
File1.Pattern = ("*.bmp;*.wmf;*.jpg;*.gif")
Else
File1.Pattern = ("*.*")

End If

If Right(File1.Path, 1) <> "\" Then
filenam = File1.Path + "\" + File1.FileName
Else
filenam = File1.Path + File1.FileName
End If

End Sub
□

Private Sub show_Click()
'To show the selected graphics file
If Right(File1.Path, 1) <> "\" Then
filenam = File1.Path + "\" + File1.FileName
Else
filenam = File1.Path + File1.FileName
End If
Picture1.Picture = LoadPicture(filenam)

End Sub
```

The Code for Second Method

The second way is much easier to program, you only need to insert an image control, a common dialog box and an icon that resembles on opened file. You need to set the stretchable property of the image control to true. The procedure to open the common dialog box to browse the image files as well as to load the selected picture into the image control is

```
CommonDialog1.Filter =
"Bitmaps(*.BMP)|*.BMP|Metafiles(*.WMF)|*.WMF|Jpeg
Files(*.jpg)|*.jpg|GIF Files(*.gif)|*.gif|Icon Files(*.ico)|*.ico|All
Files(*.*)|*.*"

CommonDialog1.ShowOpen

Picture1.Picture = LoadPicture(CommonDialog1.FileName)
```

The filter property of the common dialog box uses the format as shown below

```
Bitmaps(*.BMP)|*.BMP
```

To specify the file type, and uses the pipeline | to separate different file types.

Visual Basic supports most of the picture formats namely bmp, wmf, jpg, gif, ico(icon) and cur(cursor) files.

The command CommonDialog1.ShowOpen is to open the common dialog box and the command

```
Picture1.Picture = LoadPicture (CommonDialog1.FileName)
```

is to load the selected picture file into the picture box.

The full code is as follows:

```
Private Sub Image1_Click()

CommonDialog1.Filter =
"Bitmaps(*.BMP)|*.BMP|Metafiles(*.WMF)|*.WMF|Jpeg
Files(*.jpg)|*.jpg|GIF Files(*.gif)|*.gif|Icon Files(*.ico)|*.ico|All
Files(*.*)|*.*"

CommonDialog1.ShowOpen
```

image2.Picture = LoadPicture (CommonDialog1.FileName)

End Sub

The second way is much easier to program, you only need to insert an image control, a common dialog box and an icon that resembles on opened file. You need to set the stretchable property of the image control to true. The procedure to open the common dialog box to browse the image files as well as to load the selected picture into the image control is

```
CommonDialog1.Filter =
"Bitmaps(*.BMP)|*.BMP|Metafiles(*.WMF)|*.WMF|Jpeg
Files(*.jpg)|*.jpg|GIF Files(*.gif)|*.gif|Icon Files(*.ico)|*.ico|All
Files(*.*)|*.*"

CommonDialog1.ShowOpen

Picture1.Picture = LoadPicture(CommonDialog1.FileName)
```

The filter property of the common dialog box uses the format as follows:

```
Bitmaps(*.BMP)|*.BMP
```

to specify the file type and uses the pipeline | to separate different file types.

Visual Basic supports most of the picture formats namely bmp, wmf, jpg, gif, ico(icon) and cur(cursor) files. The command CommonDialog1.ShowOpen is to open the common dialog box and the command

```
Picture1.Picture = LoadPicture (CommonDialog1.FileName)
```

is to load the selected picture file into the picture box.

The full code is as follows:

```
Private Sub Image1_Click()
```

CommonDialog1.Filter = "Bitmaps(*.BMP)|*.BMP|Metafiles(*.WMF)|*.WMF|Jpeg _ Files(*.jpg)|*.jpg|GIF Files(*.gif)|*.gif|Icon Files(*.ico)|*.ico|All _ Files(*.*)|*.*"

CommonDialog1.ShowOpen

image2.Picture = LoadPicture (CommonDialog1.FileName)

End Sub

When the user clicks the opened file icon, the following dialog will appear. The user then can select the file he or she wishes to view, as shown in Figure 4.2.

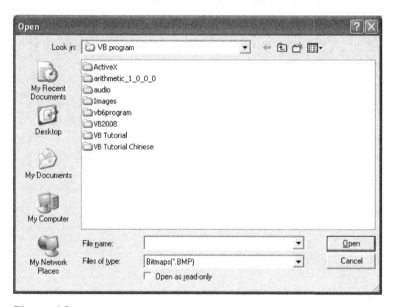

Figure 4.2

The Runtime Interface is shown in Figure 4.3

Figure 4.3

5 Multimedia Programs

In Visual Basic, you can create various multimedia applications that can play audio CD, various audio files including mp3, wav and midi files; and different types of video files such as avi, mpeg files and etc. To be able to play multimedia files or multimedia devices, you have to insert the **Microsoft Multimedia Control** into your applications that you are going to create.

However, Microsoft Multimedia Control is not included in the default toolbox. Therefore, you need to add the Microsoft Multimedia control from the components dialog box. To access the components dialog box, press Ctrl+T. Select **Microsoft Multimedia control 6.0** from the components available in the dialog box as shown in the Figure 5.1. and then press the OK button. When you close the dialog box, you will notice that the Microsoft Multimedia Control will be available in the toolbox and you can add it to the form.

Figure 5.1

5.1 Creating a DVD Player

In this program, insert the Microsoft Multimedia Control and set its properties to Visible to True as well as Play to Enabled. In addition, insert five command buttons and name as well as label them as Play, Next, Previous, Stop and Exit. Besides that, insert a label that can be used to display the current track number of the song being played. Lastly, enter the program codes.

The most important statement in this program is to set the Microsoft Multimedia Control's device type to CDAudio because it will ensure audio CDs can be played.

```
MMControl1.DeviceType = "CDAudio"
```

To display the track number of the current song being played, use the following statement:

```
trackNum.Caption = MMControl1.Track
```

The Play, Next, Previous and Stop commands can be programmed using the

```
MMControl1.Command = "Play", MMControl1.Command = "Next",
MMControl1.Command = "Prev", and MMControl1.Command = "Stop"
statement.
```

Lastly, always ensure that the Microsoft Multimedia Control is closed whenever the user closes the player. This can be achieved by using the statement

```
MMControl1.Command = "Close"
```

Under **Form1_Unload** procedure.

The Code

```vb
Private Sub Form_Load ()
'To position the page at the center
Left = (Screen.Width - Width) \ 2
Top = (Screen.Height - Height) \ 2
End Sub

Private Sub Form_Activate ()
'Load the CDPlayer
MMControl1.Notify = False
MMControl1.Wait = True
MMControl1.DeviceType = "CDAudio"
MMControl1.Command = "Open"
End Sub

Private Sub MMControl1_StatusUpdate ()
'Update the track number
trackNum.Caption = MMControl1.Track
End Sub

Private Sub Next_Click ()
MMControl1.Command = "Next"
End Sub

Private Sub Play_Click ()
MMControl1.Command = "Play"
End Sub

Private Sub Previous_Click ()
```

MMControl1.Command = "Prev"

End Sub

Private Sub Stop_Click ()

MMControl1.Command = "Stop"

End Sub

Private Sub Exit_Click ()

MMControl1.Command = "Stop"

MMControl1.Command = "Close"

End

End Sub

Private Sub Form1_unload ()

'Unload the CDPlayer

MMControl1.Command = "Close"

End Sub

The DVD Player Interface

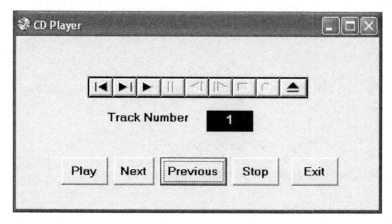

Figure 5.2

5.2 A Smart Audio Player

In the preceding section, you have programmed a DVD player. Now, by making some minor alterations, you can transform the DVD player into an audio player. This player will be created in such a way that it can search for sound files in your drives and play them.

In this project, you need to insert a ComboBox, a DriveListBox, a DirListBox, a TextBox and a FileListBox into your form. I shall briefly discuss the function of each of the above controls. Besides that, you must also insert Microsoft Multimedia Control (MMControl) in your form. You may make it visible or invisible. In this program, I choose to make it invisible so that I can use the command buttons created to control the player. The functions of the various controls are explained below:

a) The ComboBox

Displays and enables the selection of different types of files. To add items to the Combo Box, you can use the AddItem method. The items here are the extensions of different audio files.

b) The DriveListBox

The DriveListBox allows the selection of different drives in your computer.

c) The DirListBox

The DirListBox displays different directories that are available in your computer.

d) The Textbox

The Textbox displays the selected files.

e) The FileListBox

The FileListBox displays files that are available in your computer.

Relevant codes must be written to coordinate all the above controls so that the application can work properly. The program should flow in the following logical steps:

Step 1: User chooses the type of files he wants to play.

Step2: User selects the drive that might contain the relevant audio files.

Step 3: User looks into directories and subdirectories for the files specified in step1. The files should be displayed in the FileListBox.

Step 4: User selects the files from the FileListBox and clicks the Play button.

Step 5: User clicks on the Stop button to stop playing and the Exit button to end the application.

To coordinate the DriveListBox and the DirListBox, you can use the statement below, so that any change of the drives will be reflected in the directory list box.

Dir1.Path = Drive1.Drive

To coordinate the FileListBox and the DirListBox, you can use the statement below so that any change of the directories will be reflected in the File List Box.

File1.Path = Dir1.Path

To select the target file, you can use the following statements where File1.Path determines the path of the file and File1.FileName determines the file name. The file name is then assigned to the variable filename and displayed in the text box.

```
If Right (File1.Path, 1) <> "\" Then
filenam = File1.Path + "\" + File1.FileName
Else
filenam = File1.Path + File1.FileName
End If
Text1.Text = filenam
```

To select the file types, you can use the statement File1.Pattern = ("*.wav") to choose the wave audio files and the statement File1.Pattern = ("*.mid") to choose the sequencer files.

To play the selected file, use the following procedure:

```
Private Sub play_Click ()
'To play WaveAudio file or Midi File
If Combo1.ListIndex = 0 Then
MMControl1.DeviceType = "WaveAudio"
ElseIf Combo1.ListIndex = 1 Then
MMControl1.DeviceType = "Sequencer"
End If
MMControl1.FileName = Text1.Text
MMControl1.Command = "Open"
MMControl1.Command = "Play"
End Sub
```

The statement **MMControl1.DeviceType = "WaveAudio"** enables the Microsoft Multimedia Control to play Wave Audio files and the statement **MMControl1.DeviceType = "Sequencer"** enables the Microsoft Multimedia Control to play the midi files. In fact, the Microsoft Multimedia Control can play many other types of multimedia files, including Mpeg, Mp3 and Avi video files.

The statement **MMControl1.FileName = Text1.Text** plays the multimedia file displayed in the Text1 textbox. The statement **MMControl1.Command = "Open"** initiates the Microsoft Multimedia Control and the statement **MMControl1.Command = "Play"** plays the multimedia file. The statement **MMControl1.Command = "stop"** stops the Microsoft Multimedia Control from playing and finally the statement **MMControl1.Command = "Close"** closes the Microsoft Multimedia Control.

The Code

```
Private Sub Form_Load ()

'To center the Audioplayer

Left = (Screen.Width - Width) \ 2
Top = (Screen.Height - Height) \ 2
Combo1.Text = "*.wav"
Combo1.AddItem "*.wav"
Combo1.AddItem "*.mid"
Combo1.AddItem "All files"

End Sub


Private Sub Combo1_Change ()

'To determine file type

If ListIndex = 0 Then
File1.Pattern = ("*.wav")
ElseIf ListIndex = 1 Then
File1.Pattern = ("*.mid")
Else
Fiel1.Pattern = ("*.*")
End If

End Sub


Private Sub Dir1_Change ()
```

182

```
'To change directories and subdirectories (or folders and subfolders)
File1.Path = Dir1.Path
If Combo1.ListIndex = 0 Then
File1.Pattern = ("*.wav")
ElseIf Combo1.ListIndex = 1 Then
File1.Pattern = ("*.mid")
Else
File1.Pattern = ("*.*")
End If

End Sub


Private Sub Drive1_Change ()

'To change drives

Dir1.Path = Drive1.Drive

End Sub


Private Sub File1_Click ()

If Combo1.ListIndex = 0 Then
File1.Pattern = ("*.wav")
ElseIf Combo1.ListIndex = 1 Then
File1.Pattern = ("*.mid")
Else
File1.Pattern = ("*.*")
End If
If Right(File1.Path, 1) <> "\" Then
filenam = File1.Path + "\" + File1.FileName
Else
filenam = File1.Path + File1.FileName
End If
Text1.Text = filename

End Sub

Private Sub play_Click ()

'To play WaveAudio file or Midi file
```

183

```
If Combo1.ListIndex = 0 Then
MMControl1.DeviceType = "WaveAudio"
ElseIf Combo1.ListIndex = 1 Then
MMControl1.DeviceType = "Sequencer"
End If
MMControl1.FileName = Text1.Text
MMControl1.Command = "Open"
MMControl1.Command = "Play"

End Sub


Private Sub stop_Click ()

MMControl1.Command = "Stop"

 End Sub

Private Sub Exit_Click ()

MMControl1.Command = "Close"

End

End Sub
Private Sub Drive1.Change( )

Dir1.Path=Drive1.Drive

End Sub
```

Smart Audio Player Interface

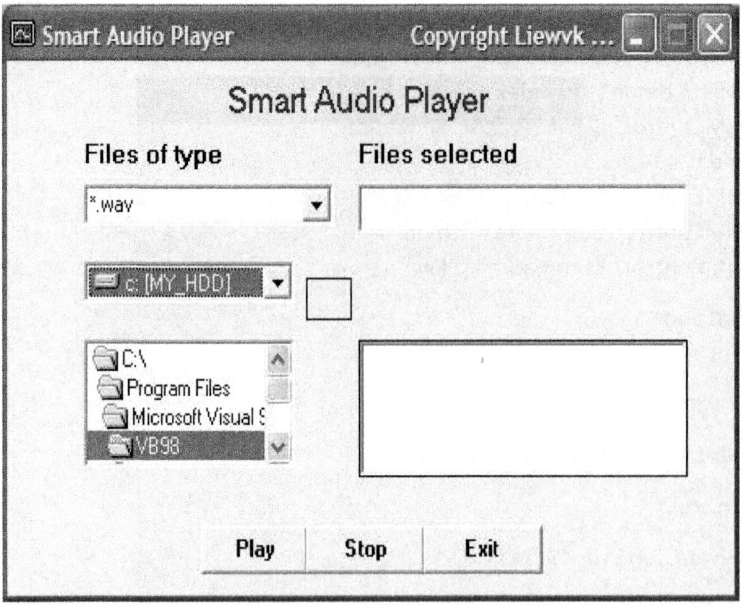
Smart Audio Player
Copyright Liewvk ...
Smart Audio Player
Files of type
Files selected
*.wav
c: [MY_HDD]
C:\
Program Files
Microsoft Visual S
VB98
Play
Stop
Exit

Figure 5.3

185

5.3 Multimedia Player

In the preceding section, you have created an audio player. Now, by making some minor modifications, you will transform the audio player into a multimedia player that can play all kinds of movie files besides audio files. This player will be created in such a way that it can search for all types of media files in your computer drives and play them.

In this project, you need to insert a ComboBox, a DriveListBox, a DirListBox, a TextBox, a FileListBox, and a picture box (for playing movies) into your form. I shall briefly discuss the function of each of the above controls. You must also insert Microsoft Multimedia Control (MMControl) in your form; you may make it visible or invisible. In my program, I choose to make it invisible so that I can use the command buttons created to control the player.

The program is similar to the audio player, but you need to add a few extra statements so that you can play the video files and also the mp3 files. First of all, you have to add two more file types with the statements **File1.Pattern = ("*.avi")** and **File1.Pattern = ("*.mpeg;*.mpg;*.mp3")** so that the Avi and Mpeg movie files as well as the mp3 files will show up in the file list box . Secondly, you have to add the statement **MMControl1.DeviceType = "AVIVideo"** so that the Microsoft Multimedia Control can play the Avi video files and **MMControl1.DeviceType = " "** so that the player can play other media files such as the mp3 files.

The Code

Private Sub Form_Load ()

Left = (Screen.Width - Width) \ 2

Top = (Screen.Height - Height) \ 2

Combo1.Text = "*.wav"

Combo1.AddItem "*.wav"

```
186

Combo1.AddItem "*.mid"

Combo1.AddItem "*.avi"

Combo1.AddItem "*.mpeg;*.mpg;*.mp3"

Combo1.AddItem "All files"

End Sub

Private Sub Combo1_Change ()

If ListIndex = 0 Then

File1.Pattern = ("*.wav")

ElseIf ListIndex = 1 Then

File1.Pattern = ("*.mid")

ElseIf ListIndex = 2 Then

File1.Pattern = ("*.avi")

ElseIf ListIndex = 3 Then

File1.Pattern = ("*.mpeg;*.mpg;*.mp3")

Else

Fiel1.Pattern = ("*.*")

End If

End Sub

Private Sub Dir1_Change ()

File1.Path = Dir1.Path

If Combo1.ListIndex = 0 Then

File1.Pattern = ("*.wav")

ElseIf Combo1.ListIndex = 1 Then

File1.Pattern = ("*.mid")

ElseIf Combo1.ListIndex = 2 Then
```

```
File1.Pattern = ("*.avi")

ElseIf Combo1.ListIndex = 3 Then

File1.Pattern = ("*.mpeg;*.mpg;*.mp3")

Else

File1.Pattern = ("*.*")

End If

End Sub


Private Sub Drive1_Change ()

Dir1.Path = Drive1.Drive

End Sub

Private Sub File1_Click ()

If Combo1.ListIndex = 0 Then

File1.Pattern = ("*.wav")

ElseIf Combo1.ListIndex = 1 Then

File1.Pattern = ("*.mid")

ElseIf Combo1.ListIndex = 2 Then

File1.Pattern = ("*.avi")

ElseIf Combo1.ListIndex = 3 Then

File1.Pattern = ("*.mpeg;*.mpg;*.mp3")

Else

File1.Pattern = ("*.*")

End If

If Right (File1.Path, 1) <> "\" Then

filenam = File1.Path + "\" + File1.FileName

Else
```

```vb
filenam = File1.Path + File1.FileName

End If

Text1.Text = filename

End Sub

Private Sub Exit_Click ()

MMControl1.Command = "Close"

End

End Sub

Private Sub Open_Click ()

If Combo1.ListIndex = 0 Then

MMControl1.DeviceType = "WaveAudio"

End If

If Combo1.ListIndex = 1 Then

MMControl1.DeviceType = "Sequencer"

End If

If Combo1.ListIndex = 2 Then

MMControl1.DeviceType = "AVIVideo"

End If

If Combo1.ListIndex = 3 Then

MMControl1.DeviceType = ""

End If

MMControl1.FileName = Text1.Text

MMControl1.Command = "Open"

End Sub

Private Sub play_Click ()
```

189

```
Timer1.Enabled = True
MMControl1.Command = "Play"
MMControl1.hWndDisplay = Picture1.hWnd
End Sub
Private Sub stop_Click ()
If MMControl1.Mode = 524 Then Exit Sub
If MMControl1.Mode <> 525 Then
MMControl1.Wait = True
MMControl1.Command = "Stop"
End If
MMControl1.Wait = True
MMControl1.Command = "Close"
End Sub
```

The Interface is shown in Figure 5.4

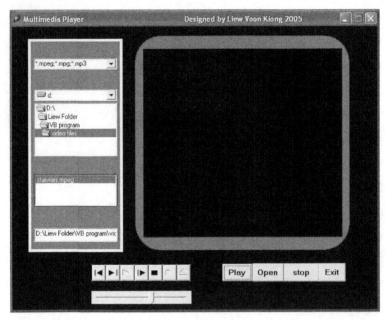

Figure 5.4

6 Tools and Utilities
6.1 BMI Calculator

Many people are obese nowadays and it is affecting their health seriously. If a person's BMI is more than 30, he or she is considered obese. You can refer to the following range of BMI values for the weight status.

- Underweight = <18.5

- Normal weight = 18.5-24.9

- Overweight = 25-29.9

- Obesity = BMI of 30 or greater

This BMI calculator is a Visual Basic program that can calculate the body mass index, or BMI of a person based on the body weight in kilogram and the body height in meter. BMI can be calculated using the formula

$$\frac{weight}{height^2}$$

*weight is measured in kg and height in meter. If you only know your weight and height in lb. and feet, then you need to convert them to the metric system.

The Code

```
Private Sub Command1_Click ()
Label4.Caption = BMI (Text1.Text, Text2.Text)
End Sub
```

Private Function BMI (height, weight)

BMIValue = (weight) / (height ^ 2)

BMI = Format (BMIValue, "0.00")

End Function

The Interface is shown in Figure 5.5

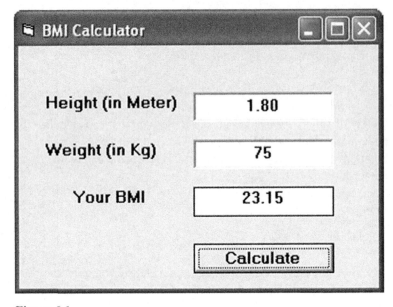

Figure 6.1

193

6.2 Calculator

This is a typical calculator that consists of the number buttons, the operator buttons, and some additional buttons such as the memory button and the clear button.

To design the interface, you need to insert 25 command buttons, and one label that functions as the display panel. The number buttons from 1 to 9 are grouped together as a control array and named as ButtonNum while 0 is a standalone command and named as Bzero. The four basic operators are also grouped together as a control array and named as Operator. Other buttons are named appropriately according to their functions. The label is named as panel.

One of the most important procedures in the program is to control the display on the panel. The procedure is

```
Private Sub ButtonNum_Click(Index As Integer)
If Num_of_digit > 0 Then
If Num_of_digit < 30 Then
panel. Caption = panel.Caption + Right$(Str(Index), 1)
Num_of_digit = Num_of_digit + 1
End If
Else
panel.Caption = Right$(Str(Index), 1)
Num_of_digit = 1
End If
CheckValue
End Sub
```

The Num_of_digit is a variable that is used to check the number of digits that appear on the display panel. The procedure will ensure that if the number of digits is more than one, the preceding digit will be pushed to the left and the succeeding digit will remain on the right. However, if the number of digits is zero, the digit clicked will just appear on the rightmost position of the panel.

Another important procedure is the procedure to perform the calculations. This can be achieved through the Operator and the Equal sub procedures. The Operator sub procedure is as follows:

```
Private Sub Operator_Click(Index As Integer)
CheckValue
If Index = 11 Then
a = displayValue
key = 1
ElseIf Index = 12 Then
b = displayValue
key = 2
ElseIf Index = 13 Then
c = displayValue
key = 3
ElseIf Index = 14 Then
d = displayValue
key = 4
ElseIf Index = 15 Then
f = displayValue
key = 5
End If
Num_of_digit = 0
newNumber = True
```

195

End Sub

This procedure ensures that when a operator button is pressed, the variable key is assigned a number so that the program knows which operator is being pressed. The calculation is then executed using the Equal sub procedure which is shown below:

```
Private Sub Equal_Click()
CheckValue
If newNumber = True Then
If key = 1 Then
e = displayValue + a
ElseIf key = 2 Then
e = b - displayValue
ElseIf key = 3 Then
e = displayValue * c
ElseIf key = 5 Then
e = (f * displayValue) / 100
ElseIf key = 4 And displayValue <> 0 Then
e = d / displayValue
Else
GoTo error
End If
If Abs(e) < 1 Then
panel.Caption = Format(e, "General Number")
Else
panel.Caption = Str(e)
```

```
End If

Else

panel.Caption = displayValue

End If

GoTo finish

error: panel.Caption = "E"

finish:

Num_of_digit = 0

newNumber = False

End Sub
```

The displayValue is the value that is displayed on the panel and this value is checked through the CheckValue sub procedure. The statements

```
If Abs(e) < 1 Then

panel.Caption = Format(e, "General Number")

Else

panel.Caption = Str(e)

End If
```

are to ensure that when the absolute value is less than 0, the zero appears in front of the decimal point, for example, 0.5 instead of just .5. The whole program is shown overleaf.

The Code

```vb
Option Explicit
Dim Num_of_digit As Integer
Dim key As Integer
Dim displayValue As Variant
Dim a, b, c, d, e, f, g As Variant
Dim memo As Variant

Dim newNumber As Boolean
Private Sub BZero_Click(Index As Integer)
If Num_of_digit > 0 Then
panel.Caption = panel.Caption + "0"
Else
panel.Caption = "0"
Num_of_digit = Num_of_digit + 1
End If
CheckValue

End Sub
Sub CheckValue()
displayValue = Val(panel.Caption)
End Sub

Private Sub ButtonNum_Click(Index As Integer)
If Num_of_digit > 0 Then
If Num_of_digit < 30 Then
panel.Caption = panel.Caption + Right$(Str(Index), 1)
Num_of_digit = Num_of_digit + 1
```

198

```vb
End If
Else
panel.Caption = Right$(Str(Index), 1)
Num_of_digit = 1
End If
CheckValue

End Sub
Private Sub Clear_Click()
panel.Caption = "0"
displayValue = "0"
Num_of_digit = 0
End Sub

Private Sub ClearAll_Click()
panel.Caption = "0"
displayValue = "0"
memo = 0
End Sub


Private Sub Equal_Click()


CheckValue
If newNumber = True Then
If key = 1 Then
e = displayValue + a
ElseIf key = 2 Then
```

```vb
e = b - displayValue
ElseIf key = 3 Then
e = displayValue * c
ElseIf key = 5 Then
e = (f * displayValue) / 100
ElseIf key = 4 And displayValue <> 0 Then
e = d / displayValue
Else
GoTo error
End If
If Abs(e) < 1 Then
panel.Caption = Format(e, "General Number")
Else
panel.Caption = Str(e)
End If
Else
panel.Caption = displayValue
End If
GoTo finish
error: panel.Caption = "E"
finish:
Num_of_digit = 0
newNumber = False
End Sub
Private Sub MemoCancel_Click()
memo = 0
```

```vb
End Sub

Private Sub Memory_Click()

CheckValue

memo = displayValue

Num_of_digit = 0

End Sub


Private Sub Operator_Click(Index As Integer)

CheckValue

If Index = 11 Then

a = displayValue

key = 1

ElseIf Index = 12 Then

b = displayValue

key = 2

ElseIf Index = 13 Then

c = displayValue

key = 3

ElseIf Index = 14 Then

d = displayValue

key = 4

ElseIf Index = 15 Then

f = displayValue

key = 5

End If

Num_of_digit = 0
```

```
newNumber = True

End Sub

Private Sub Plus_minus_Click()

CheckValue

g = -1 * displayValue

displayValue = g

panel.Caption = Str(displayValue)

CheckValue

End Sub

Private Sub Poin_Click()

Static point_lock As Integer

If point_lock = 0 And Num_of_digit < 20 Then

panel.Caption = panel.Caption + "."

Num_of_digit = Num_of_digit + 1

End If

CheckValue

End Sub

Private Sub Recall_Click()

panel.Caption = Str(memo)

End Sub

Private Sub SqRoot_Click()

CheckValue

If displayValue >= 0 Then

panel.Caption = Str(Sqr(displayValue))

Else

panel.Caption = "E"
```

End If

Num_of_digit = 0

End Sub

Private Sub Summation_Click()

CheckValue

memo = memo + displayValue

Num_of_digit = 0

End Sub

The Interface is shown in Figure 5.6

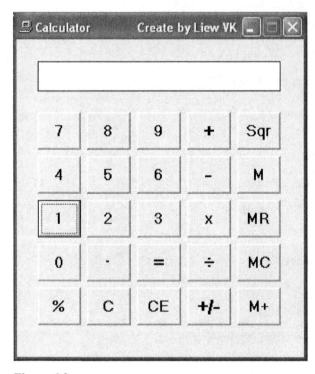

Figure 6.2

6.3 Digital Clock

Visual Basic programming is so simple that sometimes you just need to write a one line code to create a wonderful tiny little but nice application. For example, you can write a one-line code to create a digital clock.

In this program, you must insert a timer control into the form. Then go to the properties window to set the timer's interval value to 1000 so that Visual Basic updates the time every 1000 milliseconds, or once a second. Other properties that you ought to set are to change the caption such as "My Clock" and to set Form1's MaxButton to false so that it cannot be resized by the user.

Now, double click the timer and enter the one line code as follows:

```
Private Sub Timer1_Timer()
    Label1.Caption = Time
End Sub
```

The Design Interface

Figure 6.3

The Runtime Interface is shown in Figure 5.8.

Figure 6.4

6.4 Polling System

Survey and polling tools are often used in marketing or politics to assess ratings for some services or products. Polling tools be in many forms, some just use a simple dichotomous scale of Yes and No, or a more complex Likert Scale that consists of three or more choices. You can create Polling tool in Visual Basic easily by using the option buttons. In our program, the users are given five choices, Excellent, Very Good, Good, Satisfactory and Bad. The results are presented in frequency and percentage, respectively.

In this example, you can include a graphical display of the percentages of the five scores using the Line method. The syntax to draw the rectangular bars in a picture box is

Picture1.Line (x1, y1)-(x2, y2), color, BF

Where (x1, y1) is the coordinates of the upper left corner of the bar and (x2, y2) is the coordinates of the lower right corner of the bar.

To show the bar length according to the percentage, you can use a certain value to multiply the decimal value of each score and put it under x2.

Finally, you can use the Picture1.Cls method to clear the picture box to refresh the drawing.

The Code

```
Dim total, Excel_total, VG_total, G_total, Sat_total, Bad_total As
Integer
Dim Excel_percent, VG_percent, G_percent, Sat_percent, Bad_percent
As _ Single
Dim done As Boolean

Private Sub cmd_Vote_Click()

Picture1.Cls
If Option_Excel.Value = True Then
```

```
Excel_total = Excel_total + 1
Lbl_ExcelTotal = Excel_total
ElseIf Option_VG.Value = True Then
VG_total = VG_total + 1
Lbl_VGTotal = VG_total
ElseIf Option_G.Value = True Then
G_total = G_total + 1
Lbl_GTotal = G_total
ElseIf Option_Sat.Value = True Then
Sat_total = Sat_total + 1
Lbl_SatTotal = Sat_total
ElseIf Option_Bad.Value = True Then
Bad_total = Bad_total + 1
Lbl_BadTotal = Bad_total
End If
total = Excel_total + VG_total + G_total + Sat_total + Bad_total
Lbl_Total = total
Excel_percent = Excel_total / total
VG_percent = VG_total / total
G_percent = G_total / total
Sat_percent = Sat_total / total
Bad_percent = Bad_total / total
Lbl_Excel.Caption = Format(Excel_percent, "Percent")
Lbl_VG.Caption = Format(VG_percent, "Percent")
Lbl_G.Caption = Format(G_percent, "Percent")
Lbl_Sat.Caption = Format(Sat_percent, "Percent")
Lbl_Bad.Caption = Format(Bad_percent, "Percent")
Picture1.Line (100, 750)-(3800 * Excel_percent, 950), vbRed, BF
Picture1.Line (100, 1450)-(3800 * VG_percent, 1650), vbMagenta, BF
Picture1.Line (100, 2150)-(3800 * G_percent, 2350), vbGreen, BF
Picture1.Line (100, 2850)-(3800 * Sat_percent, 3050), vbBlue, BF
Picture1.Line (100, 3550)-(3800 * Bad_percent, 3750), vbYellow, BF

End Sub
```

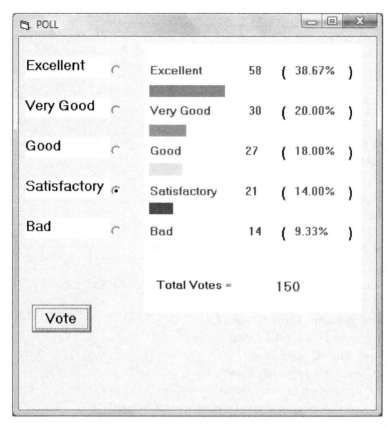

Figure 6.5

207

6.5 Digital Stopwatch

You can design a stopwatch so that it resembles a typical digital stopwatch. When the user clicks mode, he or she can select clock, date and stopwatch. When he or she selects clocks, the current time is displayed and when date is selected, the current date will be displayed. Lastly, when the user selects the stopwatch, all the digits will be set to 0 so that it can be used as a stopwatch.

In this program, you need to insert one label, three command buttons and two timers. The interval of timer1 which is used for the stopwatch and you need to set the interval at 1(1000th of a second). Timer2 will be used to display the clock and the interval will be set at 1000(or 1 second). Besides, you can also use six string variables to display the digits of the stopwatch so that you can put in the colons ":" and the decimal point. Now, you need to create a subroutine known as countime.

The code

```
Dim a As String
Dim b As String
Dim c As String
Dim x As String
Dim y As String
Dim z As String
Dim h As String
Dim m As String
Dim s As String
Dim u As String
Dim v As String

Public interval As Double
Private Sub clock_Click()

Timer1.Enabled = False
Timer2.Enabled = True
End Sub
```

208

```
Private Sub Command1_Click()

Timer1.Enabled = True
Timer1.interval = 1

End Sub

Private Sub Command2_Click()

Timer1.Enabled = False

End Sub

Private Sub Command3_Click()

Timer1.Enabled = False
a = "0"
b = "0"
c = "0"
x = "0"
y = "0"
z = "0"
u = "0"
v = "0"

h = a + b
m = c + x
s = y + z
'To set the display as "00:00:00.00"
Label1.Caption = h + ":" + m + ":" + s + "." + u + v

End Sub

Sub counttime()

If Val(v) < 9 Then
v = v + 1
Label1.Caption = a + b + ":" + c + x + ":" + y + z + "." + u + v
ElseIf Val(u) < 9 Then
v = 0
u = u + 1
```

```
Label1.Caption = a + b + ":" + c + x + ":" + y + z + "." + u + v
Elself Val(z) < 9 Then
v = 0
u = 0
z = z + 1
Label1.Caption = a + b + ":" + c + x + ":" + y + z + "." + u + v
Elself Val(y) < 5 Then
v = 0
u = 0
z = 0
y = y + 1
Label1.Caption = a + b + ":" + c + x + ":" + y + z + "." + u + v
Elself Val(x) < 9 Then
v = 0
u = 0
z = 0
y = 0
x = x + 1
Label1.Caption = a + b + ":" + c + x + ":" + y + z + "." + u + v
Elself Val(c) < 5 Then
v = 0
u = 0
z = 0
y = 0
x = 0
c = c + 1
Label1.Caption = a + b + ":" + c + x + ":" + y + z + "." + u + v
Elself Val(b) < 9 Then
v = 0
u = 0
z = 0
y = 0
x = 0
c = 0
b = b + 1
Label1.Caption = a + b + ":" + c + x + ":" + y + z + "." + u + v
Elself Val(b) < 9 Then
```

```vb
v = 0
u = 0
z = 0
y = 0
x = 0
c = 0
b = b + 1
Label1.Caption = a + b + ":" + c + x + ":" + y + z + "." + u + v
Elself Val(a) < 9 Then
v = 0
u = 0
z = 0
y = 0
x = 0
c = 0
b = 0
a = a + 1
Label1.Caption = a + b + ":" + c + x + ":" + y + z + "." + u + v
End If

End Sub

Private Sub date_Click()

Label1.Caption = Date
Timer2.Enabled = False

End Sub

Private Sub Form_Load()

a = "0"
b = "0"
c = "0"
x = "0"
y = "0"
z = "0"
u = 0
v = 0
h = a + b
```

211

```
m = c + x
s = y + z
'To set the display as "00:00:00.00"
Label1.Caption = h + ":" + m + ":" + s + "." + u + v

End Sub

Private Sub stopwc_Click()

Timer2.Enabled = False
a = "0"
b = "0"
c = "0"
x = "0"
y = "0"
z = "0"
u = "0"
v = "0"

h = a + b
m = c + x
s = y + z
Label1.Caption = h + ":" + m + ":" + s + "." + u + v

End Sub

Private Sub Timer1_Timer()

counttime

End Sub

Private Sub Timer2_Timer()

Label1.Caption = Time

End Sub
```

To add the menu items to the interface, you need to add them from the menu editor, as shown in Figure 6.6

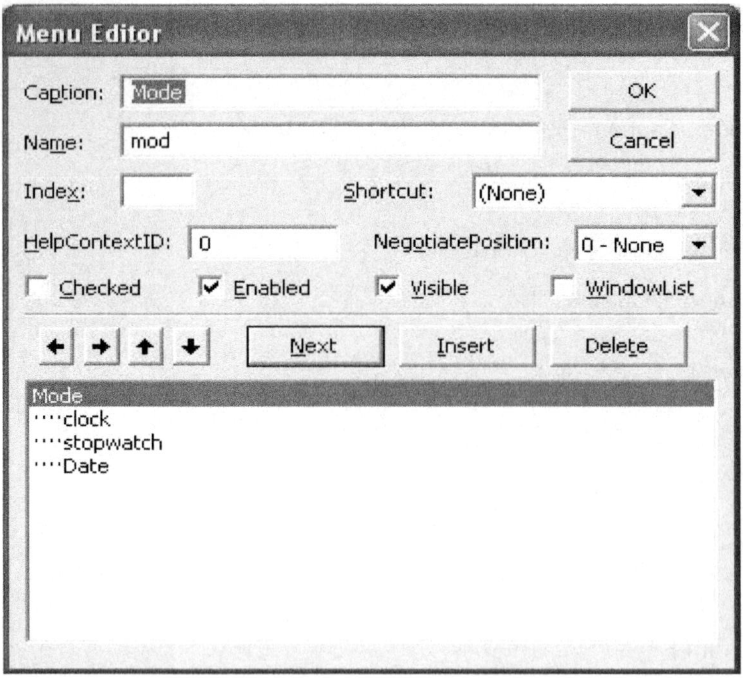

Figure 6.6

The runtime Interface is shown in Figure 6.7

Figure 6.7

214

6.6 Choice Selection Program

Very often when you visit a website, you are presented with a list of choices for you to select. Choice selection can easily be programmed in Visual Basic; the control that you can use is the check box. The status of the check box is either checked or unchecked, and the syntax is Checkbox1.Value=VbChecked or Checkbox1.Value=vbUnchecked. In the following program, you can construct a three-choice selection list. After the user made the selection, a message box will appear to display the list of selected choices

The Code

```
Private Sub Command1_Click()

If Check1.Value = vbChecked And Check2.Value = vbChecked And
Check3.Value = vbChecked Then
MsgBox ("You like Reading, Computer and Sports")
ElseIf Check1.Value = vbChecked And Check2.Value = vbChecked And
Check3.Value = vbUnchecked Then
MsgBox ("You like Reading and Computer")
ElseIf Check1.Value = vbChecked And Check2.Value = vbUnchecked
And Check3.Value = vbChecked Then
MsgBox ("You like Reading and Sports")
ElseIf Check1.Value = vbUnchecked And Check2.Value = vbChecked
And Check3.Value = vbChecked Then
MsgBox ("You like Computer and Sports")
ElseIf Check1.Value = vbChecked And Check2.Value = vbUnchecked
And Check3.Value = vbChecked Then
MsgBox ("You like Reading and Sports")
ElseIf Check1.Value = vbChecked And Check2.Value = vbUnchecked
And Check3.Value = vbUnchecked Then
MsgBox ("You like Reading only ")
ElseIf Check1.Value = vbUnchecked And Check2.Value = vbChecked
And Check3.Value = vbUnchecked Then
MsgBox ("You like computer only")
ElseIf Check1.Value = vbUnchecked And Check2.Value = vbUnchecked
```

And Check3.Value = vbChecked Then
MsgBox ("You like Sports only")
Else
MsgBox ("You have no hobby")
End If

End Sub

The Interface is shown in Figure 6.8.

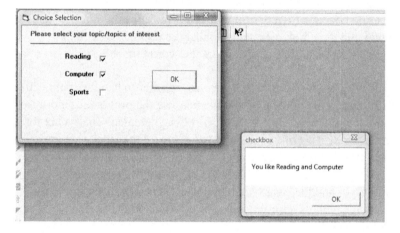

Figure 6.8

7 Database Applications
7.1 Simple Database Management System

This is a simple database management system that stores data using a text file. First, the program will check whether the text file is open or not and if the file does not exist, the program prompts the user to create the file by displaying the create button.

However, if the file is already there, the program will change the caption of the create button to open file. The program uses Append in the place of Output so that new data will be added to the end of the file instead of overwriting the old data. The program will also show the input box repeatedly so that the user can enter data continuously until he or she enters the word "finish".

The program also introduces the error handler to handle errors while reading the file or deleting the file because the program cannot read or delete the file when the file has not been created. The syntax for error handler is **On Error Goto** Label where the label is an error handling sub procedure. For example, when the program is trying to read the file when the file does not exist, it will go the label file_error and the error handling object **'err'** will display an error message with its description property which takes the format **err.description**.

The program uses the **vbCrLf** constant when reading the data so that the data will appear line by line instead of a continuous line. The vbCrLf constant is equivalent to the pressing of the Enter key (or return key) so that the next data will go to the newline. The program is using the Do…Loop to read all the data until it reaches the end of the file by issuing the command Loop While Not EOF.

217

The Code

```
Dim studentname As String
Dim intMsg As String

Private Sub Command1_Click()
'To read the file
Text1.Text = ""
Dim variable1 As String
On Error GoTo file_error
Open "C:\My Folder\sample.txt" For Input As #1
Do
Input #1, variable1
Text1.Text = Text1.Text & variable1 & vbCrLf
Loop While Not EOF(1)
Close #1

Exit Sub
file_error:
MsgBox (Err.Description)

End Sub

Private Sub Command2_Click()
'To delete the file
On Error GoTo delete_error
Kill "D:\Liew Folder\sample.txt"
Exit Sub
delete_error:
MsgBox (Err.Description)

End Sub

Private Sub create_Click()
'To create the file or open the file for new data entry
Open "D:\MyFolder\sample.txt" For Append As #1
intMsg = MsgBox("File sample.txt opened")
Do
studentname = InputBox("Enter the student Name or type finish to
```

218

```
end")
If studentname = "finish" Then
Exit Do
End If
Write #1, studentname & vbCrLf
intMsg = MsgBox("Writing " & studentname & " to sample.txt ")
Loop
Close #1
intMsg = MsgBox("File sample.txt closed")

End Sub

Private Sub Form_Load()

On Error GoTo Openfile_error
Open "D:\ MyFolder\sample.txt" For Input As #1
Close #1
Exit Sub
Openfile_error:
MsgBox (Err.Description), , "Please create a new file"
create.Caption = "Create File"

End Sub
```

The Interface is shown in Figure 7.1.

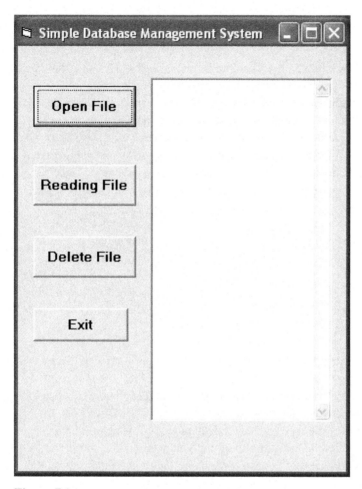

Figure 7.1

7.2 A Simple Database Application

In this example, you will create a simple database application which enables the user to browse customers' names. To create this application, insert the data control into the new form. Place the data control somewhere at the bottom of the form. Name the data control as data_navigator. To be able to use the data control, you must connect it to any database. You can create a database file using any database application, but I suggest you use the database files that come with VB6. Let us select **NWIND.MDB** as the database file.

To connect the data control to this database, double-click the **DatabaseName** property in the properties window and select the above file. Next, double-click on the **RecordSource** property to select the customers' table from the database. You can also change the caption of the data control to anything but I use "Click to browse Customers" here. After that, insert a label and change its caption to Customer Name.

Finally, insert another label and name it as cus_name and leave the label empty as customers' names will appear here when the user clicks the arrows on the data control. You need to bind this label to the data control for the application to work. To do this, open the label's **DataSource** and select data_navigator, which will appear automatically. One more thing that you need to do is to bind the label to the correct field so that data in the field will appear on the label. To do this, open the **DataField** property and select ContactName. Now, press F5 and run the program. You should be able to browse all the customers' names by clicking the arrows on the data control, as shown in Figure 7.2.

Figure 7.2

Now you shall modify the same application to make it a little more advanced database management system. The data control supports some methods that are useful in manipulating the database, for example, moving the pointer to a certain location. The following are some of the commands that you can use to move the pointer around.

' Move to the first

recorddata_navigator.RecordSet.MoveFirst

' Move to the last record

data_navigator.RecordSet.MoveLast

222

' Move to the next record

data_navigator.RecordSet.MoveNext

' Move to the first record

data_navigator.RecordSet.Previous

*note: data_navigator is the name of the data control

Now, insert four command buttons and label them as First Record, Next Record, Previous Record and Last Record. They will be used to navigate the database without using the data control. You still need to retain the same data control (from example in lesson 19) but set the property Visible to False so that users will not see the data control but use the buttons instead to browse through the database. Double-click on the command button and enter the code below:

```
Private Sub CmdMoveFirst_Click ()

dtaBooks.Recordset.MoveFirst

End Sub

Private Sub CmdMoveNext_Click ()

    dtaBooks.Recordset.MoveNext

End Sub

Private Sub CmdMovePrev_Click ()

dtaBooks.Recordset.MovePrevious

End Sub

Private Sub CmdMoveLast_Click ()

dtaBooks.Recordset.MoveLast

End Sub
```

Run the application and you will obtain the interface as shown in

Figure 7.3 and you will be able to browse the database using the four command buttons.

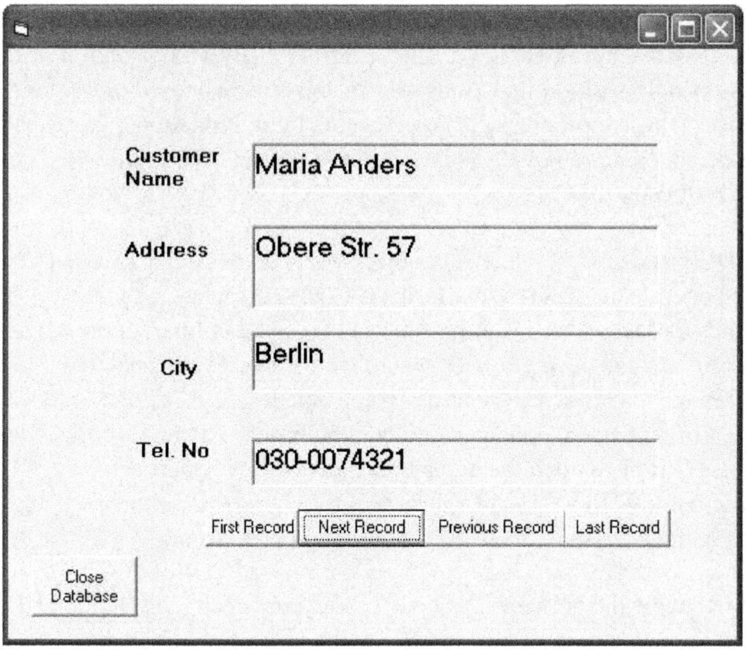

Figure 7.3

224

7.3 A Library Management System

You have learned how to build Visual Basic database applications using data control. However, data control is only a basic tool, it works only with limited kinds of data and must work strictly in the Visual Basic environment. To overcome these limitations, you can use a much more powerful data control in Visual Basic known as ADO control.

ADO stands for ActiveX data object. As ADO is ActiveX-based, it can operate on different platforms. Besides, it can access many kinds of data such as web-based data displayed in Internet browsers, email text and even graphics other than the usual relational and non-relational database information. To be able to use ADO data control, you need to insert it into the toolbox. To do this, simply press Ctrl+T to open the components dialog box and select Microsoft ActiveX Data Control 6. From here you can proceed to build the ADO-based **Library Management System.**

First, name the new form as FormLibrary and change its caption to Library Management System. Secondly, insert the ADO data control and name it as adoBooks and change its caption to book. Next, insert the necessary labels, text boxes and command buttons. The runtime interface of this program is shown in Figure 7.4; it allows adding and deleting as well as updating and browsing of data.

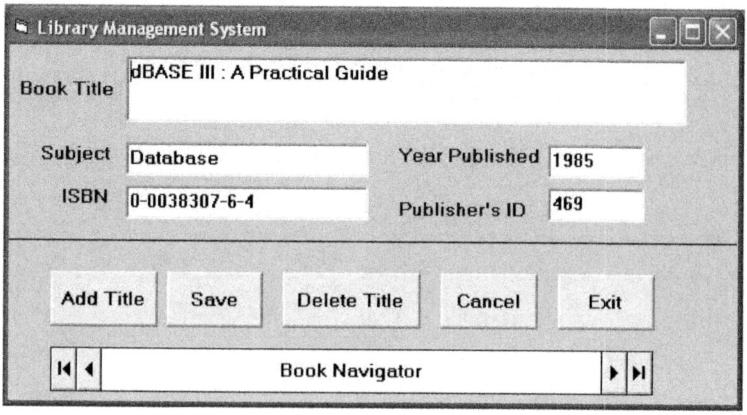

Figure 7:4

The properties of all the controls are listed in the Table 7.1.

Table 7.1

Object	Property
Form	Name : FormLibrary Caption: Book Titles -Library Management System
ADO	Name :AdoLibrary
Label1	Name : Titlelbl Caption: Book Title
Label2	Name: Subjectlbl Caption : Subject :Year Published:
Label3	Name: Yearlbl Caption : Year Published

Label 4	Name : ISBNlbl
	Caption :ISBN
Labe5	Name : PublDlbl
	Caption :Publisher's ID:
Text1	Name : Titletxt
	DataField :Title
	DataSource :AdoLibrary
Text3	Name: YearTxt
	DataField :Year Published
	DataSource: AdoLibrary
Text3	Name : ISBNTxt
	DataField :ISBN
	DataSource : AdoLibrary
Text4	Name: Pubtxt
	DataField : PublD
	DataSource: AdoLibrary
Text2	Name : Subject Txt
	DataField : Subject
	DataSource: AdoLibrary
Command Button1	Name :save
	Caption :Save
Command Button2	Name : add

	Caption: Add
Command Button3	Name: delete Caption: Delete
Command Button4	Name : cancel Caption :&Cancel
Command Button5	Name: exit Caption :Exit

To be able to access and manage a database, you need to connect the ADO data control to a database file. You will use the access database file **BIBLIO.MDB** that comes with VB6. To connect ADO to this database file, follow the steps below:

a) Click on the ADO control on the form and open up the properties window.

b) Click on the **ConnectionString** property and the following dialog box will appear.

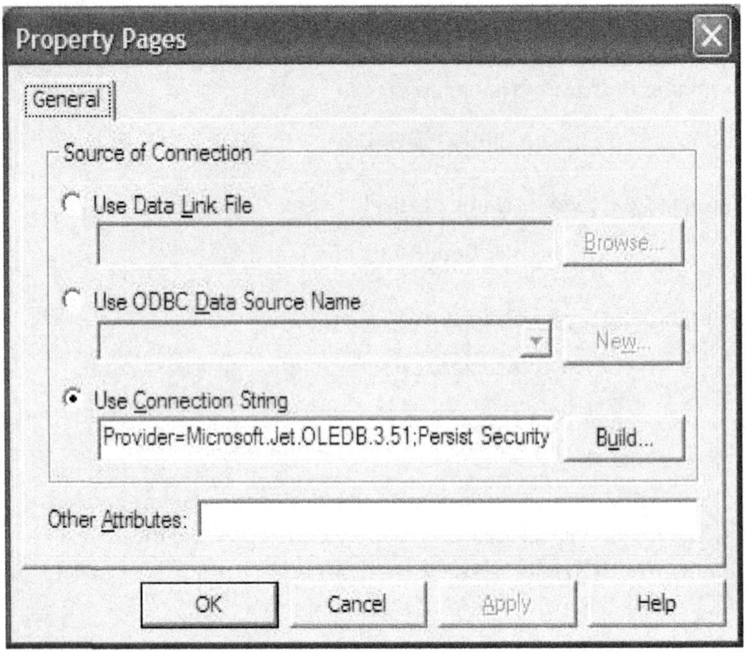

228

Figure 7.5

When the dialog box appears, select Use Connection String. Next, click build and at the Data Link dialog box, double-click the option labelled **Microsoft Jet 3.51 OLE DB provider**, as shown in Figure 7.6.

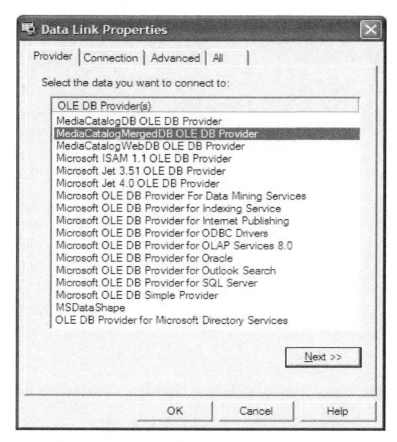

Figure 7.6

After that, click the Next button to select the file **BIBLO.MDB**. You can click on Test Connection to ensure that the connection to the database file is working. Click OK to finish the connection. Finally, click on the **RecordSource** property and set the command type to **adCmd** Table and Table name to **Titles**.

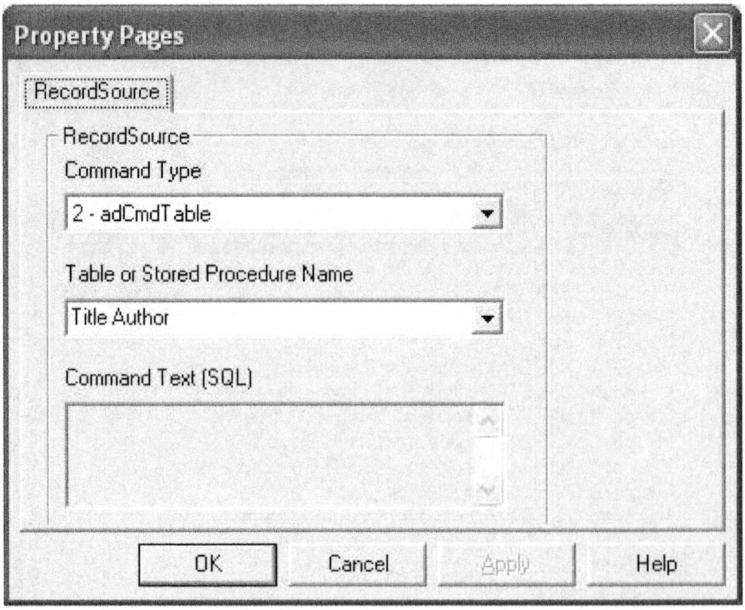

230

Figure 7.7

Now, you need to write codes for all the command buttons, after which you can make the ADO control invisible.

For the Save button, the procedure code is as follows:

```
Private Sub save_Click()

On Error GoTo errSave

AdoLibrary.Recordset.Fields("Title") = TitleTxt.Text

AdoLibrary.Recordset.Fields("Year Published") = YearTxt.Text

AdoLibrary.Recordset.Fields("ISBN") = ISBNTxt.Text

AdoLibrary.Recordset.Fields("PubID") = PubTxt.Text

AdoLibrary.Recordset.Fields("Subject") = SubjectTxt.Text

AdoLibrary.Recordset.Update

Exit Sub
```

231

```
errSave:

MsgBox (Err.Description)

End Sub
```

For the Add button, the procedure code is as follows:

```
Private Sub Add_Click()

On Error GoTo addErr

AdoLibrary.Recordset.AddNew

Exit Sub

addErr:

MsgBox (Err.Description)

End Sub
```

For the Delete button, the procedure code is as follows:

```
Private Sub delete_Click()

Confirm = MsgBox("Are you sure you want to delete this record?",
vbYesNo, "Deletion Confirmation")

If Confirm = vbYes Then

On Error GoTo deleteErr

AdoLibrary.Recordset.delete

MsgBox "Record Deleted!",, "Message"

Else

MsgBox "Record Not Deleted!", , "Message"

End If

Exit Sub
```

232

deleteErr:

MsgBox (Err.Description), , "Empty record, please enter all the info"

End Sub

For the Cancel button, the procedure is as follows:

Private Sub cancel_Click()

TitleTxt.Text = ""

YearTxt.Text = ""

PubTxt.Text = ""

ISBNTxt.Text = ""

SubjectTxt.Text = ""

End Sub

Now you shall enhance the library management system by adding some new features such as a welcome dialog, a registration dialog, a login dialog, and SQL search capabilities. The registration dialog will accept users' registrations and the login dialog will handle a login command that requires the user to enter a password, thus enhancing the security aspect of the database management system. Basically, the application will constitute a welcome menu, a registration menu, a login menu, and the main database menu. The sequence of the dialogs is illustrated in the flowchart below:

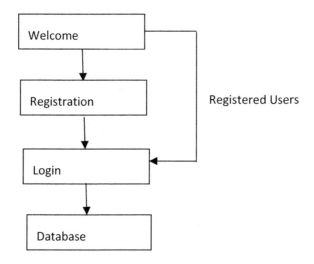

First, insert a form and design it as the Welcome menu as shown in the Figure 7.8. In this form, insert three command buttons and set their properties as listed in Table 7.2.

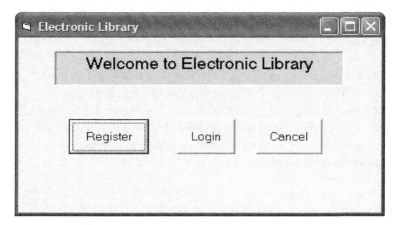

Figure 7.8

234

Table 7.2

Object	Name	Caption
Form name	main_menu	Electronic Library
command button 1	cmdRegister	Register
command button 2	cmdLogin	Login
command button 3	cmdCancel	Cancel

The procedure code for the welcome menu is shown below:

```
Private Sub cmdLogin_Click ()

main_menu.Hide
Login_form.Show

End Sub
Private Sub cmdRegister_Click ()

main_menu.Hide
Register. Show

End Sub
```

If a new user clicks the Register button, the registration form will appear. This registration form consists of two text boxes, three command buttons and an ADO control. Their properties are listed in the Table 7.3 and the interface is shown Figure 7.9. Note that the PasswordChar of the Text2 textbox is set as * to hide the real passwords from others.

Table 7.3

Object	Property
Form	Name :Register Caption: Registration Form
Text1	Name: txtName
Text2	Name: txtpassword
Text2	PasswordChar : *
command button 1	Name :cmdConfirm Caption: Confirm
command button 2	Name: cmdClear Caption: Clear
command button 3	Name: cmdCancel Caption: Cancel
ADO control name	Name :UserInfo

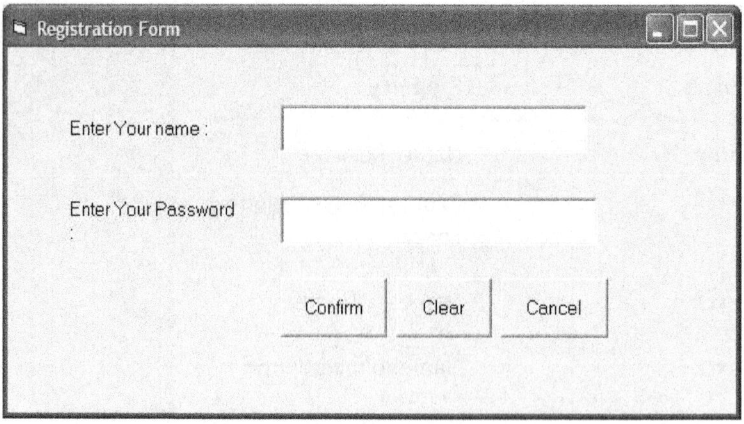

236

Figure 7.9

To connect the ADO to a database, you must create a database file in Microsoft Access. The database file must contain at least two fields, one for the username and the other one for the password. The procedure code for the registration form is as follows:

```
Private Sub cmdClear_Click ( )

txtName.Text = ""

txtpassword.Text = ""

End Sub

Private Sub cmdConfirm_Click ()

UserInfo.Recordset.Fields ("username") = txtName.Text
UserInfo.Recordset.Fields ("password") = txtpassword.Text
UserInfo.Recordset.Update
Register. Hide
Login_form.Show

End Sub
Private Sub Form_Load ()

UserInfo.Recordset.AddNew

End Sub
```

The login dialog is illustrated in Figure 7.10.

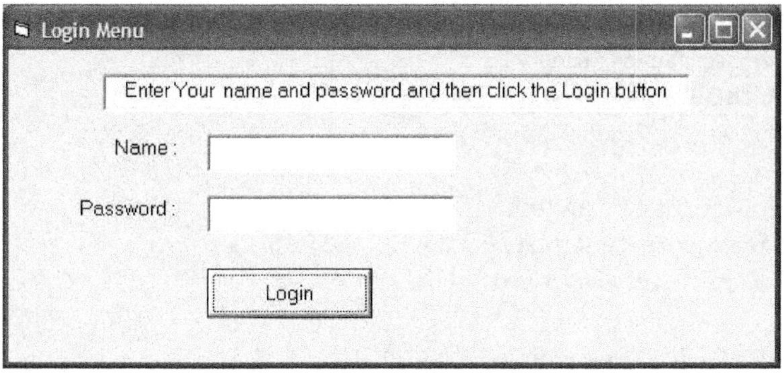

Figure 7.10

There are two text boxes and a command button on the Login form. Their properties are set as in Table 7.4.

Table 7.4

Object	Property
Text1	Name: txtName
Text2	Name: txtpassword
	PasswordChar *
Command button 1	Name: cmdLogin
	Caption: Login
Form name	Name: Login form
	Caption: Login Menu

238

The Code

```
Private Sub cmdLogin_Click()

Dim usrname As String
Dim psword As String
Dim usernam As String
Dim pssword As String
Dim Msg As String

Register.UserInfo.Refresh
usrname = txtName.Text
psword = txtpassword.Text

Do Until Register.UserInfo.Recordset.EOF
If Register.UserInfo.Recordset.Fields ("username").Value = usrname
And Register.UserInfo.Recordset.Fields ("password").Value = psword
Then
Login_form.Hide
frmLibrary.Show

Exit Sub
Else
Register.UserInfo.Recordset.MoveNext
End If
Loop
Msg = MsgBox ("Invalid password, try again!", vbOKCancel)
If (Msg = 1) Then
Login_form.Show
txtName.Text = ""
txtpassword = ""
Else
End
 End If

End Sub
```

239

Now you shall modify the library management system interface and add even more features to it. You shall add the following components:

- Database navigation buttons

- Microsoft DataGrid Control 6.0

- Search Box

The properties of the command buttons are set as shown in the table on next page.

Table 7.5

Object	Property
Command button 1	Name: cmdFirst Caption: First Record
Command button 2	Name: cmdNext Caption: Next Record
Command button 3	Name: cmdPrevious Caption: Previous Record
Command button 4	Name: cmdLast Caption: Last Record
Command button 5	Name: cmdViewAll Caption: View All Records

Label1	Name: LblSearch
	Caption: Search
Option Button1	Name: Opt_ISBN
	Caption: ISBN
Option Button 2	Name: Opt_Author
	Caption: Author
Option Button 3	Name: Opt_Title
	Caption: Title
Microsoft DataGrid Control 6.0	Name: DataLibrary

The code for the navigation buttons is as follows:

```
Private Sub cmdFirst_Click()

AdoLibrary.Recordset.MoveFirst

End Sub

Private Sub cmdLast_Click()

AdoLibrary.Recordset.MoveLast

End Sub

Private Sub cmdNew_Click()

AdoLibrary.Recordset.AddNew

End Sub

Private Sub cmdNext_Click()
```

241

```
AdoLibrary.Recordset.MoveNext

End Sub


Private Sub cmdPrevious_Click()

AdoLibrary.Recordset.MovePrevious

End Sub
```

To add search and query capability to the library management system, you can use SQL (Structures Query Language). To be able to use SQL with Visual Basic, you must connect the Visual Basic application to the database library.mdb using the following statements under the Form_Load procedure:

```
'To connect to MS Access database library.mdb

AdoLibrary.ConnectionString = "
Provider=Microsoft.Jet.OLEDB.4.0;Data Source=C:\My Documents\VB
Program\library.mdb;Persist Security Info=False"

AdoLibrary.RecordSource = "SELECT * FROM book"

AdoLibrary.Refresh

Set DataLibrary.DataSource = AdoLibrary

AdoLibrary.Refresh
```

*You must change the path of your database file to the actual path of the database file in your computer.

The code for SQL queries based on ISBN, author and book title is as follows:

```
Dim SearchString As String

SearchString = TxtSearch.Text

'Search for ISBN that is same as SearchString
```

If Opt_ISBN.Value = True Then

AdoLibrary.RecordSource = "SELECT * FROM book WHERE ISBN='" & SearchString & "'"

ElseIf Opt_Author.Value = True Then

'Search for author name that starts with first alphabet of SearchString

AdoLibrary.RecordSource = "SELECT * FROM book WHERE Author Like '" & SearchString & "%'"

ElseIf Opt_Title.Value = True Then

'Search for Title that starts with first alphabet of SearchString

AdoLibrary.RecordSource = "SELECT * FROM book WHERE Title Like '" & SearchString & "%'"

Explanations:

SELECT * means select ALL the records, FROM means to select information from a certain table, WHERE is the keyword that set the conditions of the query while LIKE and % are used together to search for information that begins the with first alphabet of SearchSrting

The Full code for the SQL search and the DataGrid is as follows:

Private Sub cmdSearch_Click()

Dim SearchString As String

SearchString = TxtSearch.Text

If Opt_ISBN.Value = True Then

AdoLibrary.RecordSource = "SELECT * FROM book WHERE ISBN='" & SearchString & "'"

243

```vb
ElseIf Opt_Author.Value = True Then

AdoLibrary.RecordSource = "SELECT * FROM book WHERE Author Like
'" & SearchString & "%'"

ElseIf Opt_Title.Value = True Then

AdoLibrary.RecordSource = "SELECT * FROM book WHERE Title Like '"
& SearchString & "%'"

End If

AdoLibrary.Refresh

'To reset the column width of datagrid DataLibrary

With DataLibrary

.Columns(0).Width = 2200

.Columns(1).Width = 4500

.Columns(2).Width = 2800

.Columns(3).Width = 2000

.Columns(4).Width = 800

.Columns(5).Width = 1500

End With

End Sub


Private Sub CmdViewAll_Click()

AdoLibrary.RecordSource = "SELECT * FROM book"

AdoLibrary.Refresh

'To reset the column width of datagrid DataLibrary

With DataLibrary

.Columns(0).Width = 2200

.Columns(1).Width = 4500

.Columns(2).Width = 2800
```

```vb
.Columns(3).Width = 2000

.Columns(4).Width = 800

.Columns(5).Width = 1500

End With

End Sub

Private Sub Form_Load()
'To connect to MS Access database library.mdb

AdoLibrary.ConnectionString = "
Provider=Microsoft.Jet.OLEDB.4.0;Data Source=C:\ My Documents\ VB
Program\library.mdb;Persist Security Info=False"

AdoLibrary.RecordSource = "SELECT * FROM book"

AdoLibrary.Refresh

Set DataLibrary.DataSource = AdoLibrary

AdoLibrary.Refresh


'To Set the alignment of the window to center of screen

Left = (Screen.Width - Width) \ 2

Top = (Screen.Height - Height) \ 2
'To set the alignment of the datagrid to centre of form

DataLibrary.Left = (Form1.Width - DataLibrary.Width) \ 2
'To set the column width of datagrid DataLibrary

With DataLibrary

.Columns(0).Width = 2200

.Columns(1).Width = 4500

.Columns(2).Width = 2800

.Columns(3).Width = 2000
```

245

.Columns(4).Width = 800

.Columns(5).Width = 1500

End With

End Sub

The Interface

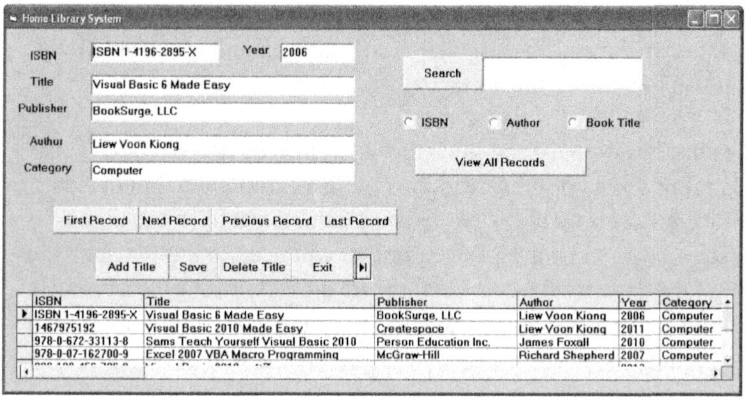

Figure 7.11

7.4 Inventory Management System

All businesses involve inventory and need to manage it efficiently to ensure smooth running of the business activities and profitability. To manage inventory efficiently, business owners need to develop a good inventory management system. Building a sound inventory management system usually incurs high cost. Fortunately, you can use Visual Basic 6 to build an inventory management system which does not require big capital; you can do it at home. In Visual Basic 6, there are several built-in database management tools which you can use to manage the data.

To start building a good inventory system, you need to have good planning. First, you must sit down with your client to get detail information about his or her businesses and establish the kind of system he or she wants. For example, you need to know what types of goods they are dealing with, the turn-over volumes, cost prices, selling prices and more. Besides that, you need to know what kind of documents the system needs to deal with like invoices, delivery orders and more.

After getting all the necessary information from your client, you can then start to build a database. Based on the number and types of products, you need to decide what are the variables or fields needed to be included in the database's tables. You shall use a hypothetical case to illustrate how to build an inventory system as shown above. Let us say our client is dealing with electrical goods.

Step 1: Creating the database tables

To design the database tables, you need to determine how many tables are needed. To keep things simple, you shall limit to two tables in our example.

The first table shall be used to store the data of the inventory or stock in hand. The second table shall be used to record stocks coming in and stocks going out.

The first table shall comprise the following fields:

- Category
- Brand
- Item Description
- Model Number
- Stock
- Unit Cost

The second table shall comprise the following fields:

- Date
- Category
- Brand
- Item Description
- Model Number
- Stock In
- Stock Out
- Unit Cost
- Total Cost

In our example, you can name the first table **Inventory** and the second table **Stock** .After designing the tables, you can then proceed to create a database that comprises the two tables. You can either use Microsoft Access to create the database or you can use the built-in **Visual Data Manager** in Visual Basic 6. Visual Data Manager can be used to create tables, add new data as well as edit data. Besides that, it can be used to modify table structure. To learn how to create database using Visual Data Manager, follow the link below:

http://www.vbtutor.net/index.php/creating-database-using-visual-data-manager/

Step 2: Inserting controls into Form

The next step is to insert some relevant controls into the form for displaying and manipulating the data of the database. The controls to be inserted are **ADO data controls**, **DataGrid controls**, **FlexGrid control** and various command buttons. DataGrid control and FlexGrid control are used to display and store the data from the database tables. On the other hand, ADO data control is used to manipulate the database such as connecting the DataGrid and FleGrid to the database.

To be able to use ADO data control, you need to insert it into the toolbox. To do this, simply press Ctrl+T to open the components dialog box and select **Microsoft ActiveX Data Control 6**. After this, you can proceed to build your ADO-based VB database applications. In our example, you need to insert two ADO data controls and name them **AdoInventory** and **AdoStock** respectively. The first is to deal with data in the Inventory table and the second is to deal with data in the Stock table. Besides, you can also insert two DataGrid controls and named them **DataInventory** and **DataStock** respectively. They are used to display the data to the user. Finally, you can insert one FlexiGrid control to store the data and to print out the data by connecting it to MS Excel spreadsheet.

Step 3: Writing the Code

After inserting the necessary controls, it is time to write code to coordinate the controls and to manipulate the data. The first most important code for our program is to connect the ADO data controls to the database when the form is loaded. It comprises SQL syntax like SELECT and FROM. The code is as follows:

```
Private Sub Form_Load()
'To connect AdoInventory to MS Access database inventory_br.mdb
AdoInventory.ConnectionString = "
Provider=Microsoft.Jet.OLEDB.4.0;Data Source=C:\My
Documents\inventory_br.mdb;Persist Security Info=False"
AdoInventory.RecordSource = "SELECT * FROM Inventory"
AdoInventory.Refresh
Set DataInventory.DataSource = AdoInventory


'To connect AdoStock to MS Access database inventory_br.mdb
AdoStock.ConnectionString = " Provider=Microsoft.Jet.OLEDB.4.0;Data
Source=C:\ My Documents\inventory_br.mdb;Persist Security
Info=False"
AdoStock.RecordSource = "SELECT * FROM Stock"
AdoStock.Refresh
Set DataStock.DataSource = AdoStock
```

Notice that you can use SQL syntax SELECT *** FROM** to select all
the data from the Inventory table and the stock table. SQL is a
powerful language that is used to manipulate databases.

The next code is to let user enter data into the **DataInventory** table
and double click to update the data as well as to calculate the total
cost. It also adds brands and categories into the **brand combo box**
and the **category combo box** respectively. The code is as follows:

```
Private Sub DataInventory_DblClick()

Dim TotalCost As Integer
If AdoInventory.Recordset.Fields("CPU") <> "" Then

TotalCost = Val(AdoInventory.Recordset.Fields("CPU")) *
Val(AdoInventory.Recordset.Fields("Stock"))
AdoInventory.Recordset.Fields("TCost") = Str(TotalCost)
Else
AdoInventory.Recordset.Fields("TCost") = ""

End If
```

```
'To load all brands into comboBrand
'To load all Categories into comboCategory
Do Until AdoInventory.Recordset.EOF
ReDim B(i), C(j) As String

B(i) = AdoInventory.Recordset.Fields("Brand")
C(j) = AdoInventory.Recordset.Fields("Category")

ComboBrand.AddItem B(i)
ComboCategory.AddItem C(j)

AdoInventory.Recordset.MoveNext
Loop
AdoInventory.Recordset.MoveFirst

End Sub
```

You can also write the code to search for the items once they are
entered into the inventory table. The code is as follows:

```
'Search for items using SQL query

Dim SearchString1, SearchString2 As String
SearchString1 = ComboBrand.Text
SearchString2 = ComboCategory.Text
If ComboBrand.Text <> "All Brands" And ComboCategory.Text <> "All
Categories" Then
AdoInventory.RecordSource = "SELECT * FROM Inventory WHERE
Brand='" & SearchString1 & "' and Category='" & SearchString2 & "'"
ElseIf ComboBrand.Text = "All Brands" And ComboCategory.Text <>
"All Categories" Then
AdoInventory.RecordSource = "SELECT * FROM Inventory WHERE
Category='" & SearchString2 & "'"
ElseIf ComboBrand.Text <> "All Brands" And ComboCategory.Text =
"All Categories" Then
AdoInventory.RecordSource = "SELECT * FROM Inventory WHERE
Brand='" & SearchString1 & "'"
```

```
ElseIf ComboBrand.Text = "All Brands" And ComboCategory.Text = "All
Categories" Then
AdoInventory.RecordSource = "SELECT * FROM Inventory"
End If
AdoInventory.Refresh
```

Next, you need to write code for entering new item in **DataStock** table. The code is as follows:

```
'To add items to Ado Stock
AdoStock.Recordset.AddNew
AdoStock.Recordset.Fields("Date") = Format(Date, "dd/mm/yyyy")
AdoStock.Recordset.Fields("Category") =
AdoInventory.Recordset.Fields("Category")
AdoStock.Recordset.Fields("Brand") =
AdoInventory.Recordset.Fields("Brand")
AdoStock.Recordset.Fields("Item Description") =
AdoInventory.Recordset.Fields("Item Description")
AdoStock.Recordset.Fields("Model Number") =
AdoInventory.Recordset.Fields("Model Number")
AdoStock.Recordset.Fields("CPU") =
AdoInventory.Recordset.Fields("CPU")
AdoStock.Recordset.Update
```

*Please note that AddNew is to allow adding new data and Update is to save data.

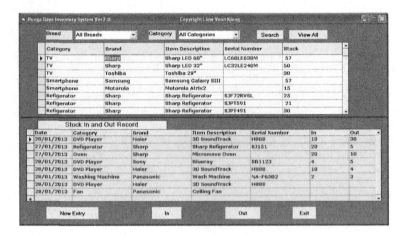

Figure 7.12

The Complete Code

'To set border styles for Excel

Private Enum ExlBorderAround

xlHairline = 1
xlMedium = -4138
xlThick = 4
xlThin = 2
xlColorIndexAutomatic = -4105
End Enum
Private Sub CmdEnd_Click()
End

End Sub

Private Sub CmdConvert_Click()

Dim hex_val As String
Dim trueVal As Double
hex_val = AdoStock.Recordset.Fields("TCost")

'To convert hexadecimal to decimal value
trueVal = CInt("&H" & hex_val)

253

```vb
Text1.Text = Str(trueVal)

End Sub

Private Sub CmdCpu_Click()

Dim CostPU As String
CostPU = InputBox("Enter Unit Cost")
AdoStock.Recordset.Fields("CPU") = Str(Val(CostPU))
AdoStock.Recordset.Fields("TCost") =
Str(Val(AdoStock.Recordset.Fields("Out")) * Val(CostPU))
AdoInventory.Recordset.Update
AdoStock.Recordset.Update

End Sub




Private Sub CmdDo_Click()
'To sum up all the values in column 9 of the Flexigrid
Dim mysum As Double
Dim nrow As Integer
Dim r As Integer
nrow = MSFlexGrid1.Rows 'To count all the rows in MSFlexiGrid1
For r = 0 To nrow - 1
mysum = mysum + Val(MSFlexGrid1.TextMatrix(r, 9))
Next

Text1.Text = Str(mysum)
'To add last line to Flexigrid table that shows total cost
MSFlexGrid1.AddItem "" & vbTab & "" & vbTab & "" & vbTab & "" &
vbTab & "" _
& vbTab & "" & vbTab & "" & vbTab & "" & vbTab & "Total Cost" &
vbTab & Str(mysum)

'Printing Delivery order Via Excel
Dim ObjExcel As Object
Dim wbk As Object
```

```vb
Dim wst As Object
Dim i%
Dim myrow, mycol, noofusedrows As Integer
Set ObjExcel = CreateObject("Excel.Application")
Set wbk = ObjExcel.Workbooks.Add
Set wst = wbk.ActiveSheet

'This Adds a new workbook, you could open the workbook from file
also

Clipboard.Clear 'Clear the Clipboard
With MSFlexGrid1
'Select Full Contents (You could also select partial content)
.Col = 0 'From first column
.Row = 0 'From first Row (header)
.ColSel = .Cols - 1 'Select all columns
.RowSel = .Rows - 1 'Select all rows
Clipboard.SetText .Clip 'Send to Clipboard
End With

With ObjExcel.Application.ActiveSheet
.Range("A1").EntireColumn.Columnwidth = 8 'Set Columnwidth for
column1=10
.Range("B1").EntireColumn.Columnwidth = 10
.Range("C1").EntireColumn.Columnwidth = 8
.Range("D1").EntireColumn.Columnwidth = 10
.Range("E1").EntireColumn.Columnwidth = 12
.Range("F1").EntireColumn.Columnwidth = 4
.Range("G1").EntireColumn.Columnwidth = 4
.Range("H1").EntireColumn.Columnwidth = 6
.Range("I1").EntireColumn.Columnwidth = 10
.Range("J1").EntireColumn.Columnwidth = 6
.Range("F1").EntireColumn.HorizontalAlignment = 2
.Range("G1").EntireColumn.HorizontalAlignment = 2
'Select Cell A1 (will paste from here, to 'different cells)
'Paste clipboard contents
.Range("A1").Select .Paste noofusedrows =
```

```vb
wst.UsedRange.Rows.Count 'To get number of used 'rows
'To set borders for the selected cells
For myrow = 2 To noofusedrows
For mycol = 1 To 10
wst.Cells(myrow, mycol).BorderAround , ExlBorderAround.xlThin,
ExlBorderAround.xlColorIndexAutomatic, vbBlack
Next
Next
'To set borders for the last row
wst.Range(.Cells(noofusedrows + 1, 1), .Cells(noofusedrows + 1,
10)).BorderAround , ExlBorderAround.xlThin,
ExlBorderAround.xlColorIndexAutomatic, vbBlack
.PrintOut 'To print out the selection
End With

End Sub


Private Sub CmdExit_Click()
    End
End Sub


Private Sub CmdIn_Click()

Dim hex_val As String
Dim StockValue
AdoStock.Recordset.Fields("In") = InputBox("Enter Stock In")
StockValue = Val(AdoStock.Recordset.Fields("In")) +
Val(AdoInventory.Recordset.Fields("Stock"))
AdoInventory.Recordset.Fields("Stock") = Str(StockValue)
AdoInventory.Recordset.Update
AdoStock.Recordset.Update

End Sub


Private Sub cmdNew_Click()
```

256

```vb
'Add new item to stock
Dim MsgInstr As Integer
MsgInstr = MsgBox("Have you selected one item from Stock List? If
YES, Click OK to Proceed", vbYesNoCancel + vbQuestion, "Select Item")
If MsgInstr = 6 Then
Timer4.Enabled = True
Else
Timer4.Enabled = False
End If

End Sub


Private Sub Cmdout_Click()

'Enter total item out
Dim StockValue
AdoStock.Recordset.Fields("Out") = InputBox("Enter Stock Out")
StockValue = Val(AdoInventory.Recordset.Fields("Stock")) -
Val(AdoStock.Recordset.Fields("Out"))
AdoInventory.Recordset.Fields("Stock") = Str(StockValue)
AdoInventory.Recordset.Update
AdoStock.Recordset.Update

End Sub


Private Sub CmdSearch_Click()

'Search for items using SQL query
Dim SearchString1, SearchString2 As String
SearchString1 = ComboBrand.Text
SearchString2 = ComboCategory.Text


If ComboBrand.Text <> "All Brands" And ComboCategory.Text <> "All
Categories" Then
AdoInventory.RecordSource = "SELECT * FROM Inventory WHERE
Brand='" & SearchString1 & "' and Category='" & SearchString2 & "'"
ElseIf ComboBrand.Text = "All Brands" And ComboCategory.Text <>
"All Categories"  Then
AdoInventory.RecordSource = "SELECT * FROM Inventory WHERE
```

```vb
Category="' & SearchString2 & "'"
ElseIf ComboBrand.Text <> "All Brands" And ComboCategory.Text =
"All Categories"  Then
AdoInventory.RecordSource = "SELECT * FROM Inventory WHERE
Brand='" & SearchString1 & "'"
ElseIf ComboBrand.Text = "All Brands" And ComboCategory.Text = "All
Categories"  Then
AdoInventory.RecordSource = "SELECT * FROM Inventory"
End If
AdoInventory.Refresh
'Formatting DataInventory (DataGrid)
With DataInventory

.Columns(0).Width = 2000 'Setting width for first column
.Columns(1).Width = 1500
.Columns(2).Width = 2500
.Columns(3).Width = 2000
.Columns(4).Width = 1200
.Columns(5).Width = 1100
.Columns(5).Caption = "Unit Cost" 'Set caption of column 8
.Columns(6).Width = 1200
.Columns(6).Caption = "Total Cost"

End With

End Sub


Private Sub CmdView_Click()

'View all items
AdoInventory.RecordSource = "SELECT * FROM Inventory"
AdoInventory.Refresh

End Sub


Private Sub Command2_Click()

AdoInventory.Recordset.Update
```

```vb
End Sub

Private Sub Command3_Click()

AdoInventory.Recordset.Delete

End Sub

Private Sub Command4_Click()

If AdoStock.Recordset.BOF = False Then
AdoStock.Recordset.Delete

Else
MsgBox ("No Item to Delete")
End If
End Sub

Private Sub Command5_Click()

AdoInventory.Refresh.Refresh

End Sub


Private Sub ComboBrand_DropDown()

Timer1.Enabled = False

End Sub

Private Sub ComboCategory_DropDown()

Dim i, j As Integer
Do Until i = ComboCategory.ListCount
For j = 1 To ComboCategory.ListCount - i - 1
If ComboCategory.List(j + i) = ComboCategory.List(i) Then

ComboCategory.RemoveItem j + i

End If
Next
```

```vb
i = i + 1
Loop

End Sub

Private Sub Command1_Click()

Dim r, nrow As Integer
Dim mysum As Double
nrow = MSFlexiGrid1.Rows
For r = 0 To nrow - 1
mysum = mysum + Val(MSFlexiGrid1.TextMatrix(nrow, 9))
Next

End Sub

Private Sub DataInventory_AfterUpdate()

Dim TotalCost As Integer
If AdoInventory.Recordset.Fields("CPU") <> "" Then
TotalCost = Val(AdoInventory.Recordset.Fields("CPU")) *
Val(AdoInventory.Recordset.Fields("Stock"))
AdoInventory.Recordset.Fields("TCost") = Str(TotalCost)
Else
AdoInventory.Recordset.Fields("TCost") = ""
End If

End Sub
Private Sub DataInventory_DblClick()

If AdoInventory.Recordset.Fields("CPU") <> "" Then
Dim TotalCost As Integer
TotalCost = Val(AdoInventory.Recordset.Fields("CPU")) *
Val(AdoInventory.Recordset.Fields("Stock"))
AdoInventory.Recordset.Fields("TCost") = Str(TotalCost)
Else
AdoInventory.Recordset.Fields("TCost") = ""
End If
'To load all brands into comboBrand
'To load all Categories into comboCategory
```

```
Do Until AdoInventory.Recordset.EOF
ReDim B(i), C(j) As String
B(i) = AdoInventory.Recordset.Fields("Brand")
C(j) = AdoInventory.Recordset.Fields("Category")
ComboBrand.AddItem B(i)
ComboCategory.AddItem C(j)
AdoInventory.Recordset.MoveNext
Loop
AdoInventory.Recordset.MoveFirst

End Sub
Private Sub DataStock_Click()

Dim TotalCost As Integer
If AdoStock.Recordset.Fields("Out") <> "" Then
TotalCost = Val(AdoStock.Recordset.Fields("CPU")) *
Val(AdoStock.Recordset.Fields("Out"))
AdoStock.Recordset.Fields("TCost") = Str(TotalCost)
End If
End Sub



Private Sub DataStock_DblClick()

'To populate the MSFlexiGrid with data from Adostock in different
columns
'whenever the user clicks the row in dataStock
MSFlexGrid1.Visible = True
Dim DateStr, CategoryStr, BrandStr, MoNumStr, ItemStr, OutStr,
InString, BranchStr, CostStr, TCostStr, AllCostStr, linetext As String
Dim AllCost As Double
DateStr = AdoStock.Recordset.Fields("Date") 'To assign the value in
Date field 'to DateStr
CategoryStr = AdoStock.Recordset.Fields("Category")
BrandStr = AdoStock.Recordset.Fields("Brand")
MoNumStr = AdoStock.Recordset.Fields("Model Number")
ItemStr = AdoStock.Recordset.Fields("Item Description")
OutStr = AdoStock.Recordset.Fields("Out")
```

```vb
InStrng = AdoStock.Recordset.Fields("In")
BranchStr = AdoStock.Recordset.Fields("Branch")
CostStr = AdoStock.Recordset.Fields("CPU")
TCostStr = AdoStock.Recordset.Fields("TCost")
AllCost = AllCost + Val(TCostStr)
AllCostStr = Str(AllCost)

linetext = DateStr & vbTab & CategoryStr & vbTab & BrandStr & vbTab & _
MoNumStr & vbTab & ItemStr & vbTab & InStrng & vbTab & OutStr & vbTab & BranchStr & vbTab & _
CostStr & vbTab & TCostStr & vbTab & AllCostStr

MSFlexGrid1.ColWidth(0) = 1200 'sets the first column width to 1000.
MSFlexGrid1.ColWidth(1) = 1500 'sets the Second column width to 2500.
MSFlexGrid1.ColWidth(2) = 1500 'sets the Third column width to 1500.
MSFlexGrid1.ColWidth(3) = 1600 'sets the Fourth column width to 1600.
MSFlexGrid1.ColWidth(4) = 2000 'sets the Fifth column width to 3000.
MSFlexGrid1.ColWidth(5) = 500 'sets the Sixth column width to 2000.
MSFlexGrid1.ColWidth(6) = 500 'sets the Seven column width to 500.
MSFlexGrid1.ColWidth(7) = 600 'sets the Seven column width to 1000.
MSFlexGrid1.ColWidth(8) = 800 'sets the Seven column width to 1000.
MSFlexGrid1.ColWidth(9) = 600 'sets the Seven column width to 1000.

'To set columns alignments
Dim ColAlign As Integer
For ColAlign = 0 To 9

MSFlexGrid1.ColAlignment(ColAlign) = flexAlignLeftTop

Next
MSFlexGrid1.AddItem linetext
AdoStock.Recordset.Update

End Sub

Private Sub Form_Load()
```

```vb
'To connect to MS Access database inventory_br.mdb
AdoInventory.ConnectionString = "
Provider=Microsoft.Jet.OLEDB.4.0;Data Source=C:\My
Documents\inventory_br.mdb;Persist Security Info=False"
AdoInventory.RecordSource = "SELECT * FROM Inventory"
AdoInventory.Refresh
Set DataInventory.DataSource = AdoInventory

'To connect to MS Access database inventory_br.mdb
AdoStock.ConnectionString = " Provider=Microsoft.Jet.OLEDB.4.0;Data
Source=C:\Documents and Settings\Voon Kiong Liew\My
Documents\Liew Folder\Bunga Raya\inventory_br.mdb;Persist
Security Info=False"
AdoStock.RecordSource = "SELECT * FROM Stock"
AdoStock.Refresh
Set DataStock.DataSource = AdoStock

'To set the alignment of the windows to centre of screen
Left = (Screen.Width - Width) \ 2
Top = (Screen.Height - Height) \ 2

'To set the alignment of the datagrid to centre of Form
DataInventory.Left = (Form1.Width - DataInventory.Width) \ 2
DataStock.Left = (Form1.Width - DataStock.Width) \ 2
'To load all brands into comboBrand
ComboBrand.Text = "All Brands"
ComboBrand.AddItem "All Brands"

'To load all Categories into comboCategory
ComboCategory.Text = "All Categories"
ComboCategory.AddItem "All Categories"

Do Until AdoInventory.Recordset.EOF
ReDim B(i), C(j) As String
B(i) = AdoInventory.Recordset.Fields("Brand")
C(j) = AdoInventory.Recordset.Fields("Category")
```

```vb
ComboBrand.AddItem B(i)
ComboCategory.AddItem C(j)
AdoInventory.Recordset.MoveNext


Loop

AdoInventory.Recordset.MoveFirst
'Formatting DataInventory (DataGrid)
With DataInventory
.Columns(0).Width = 2000 'Setting width for first column
.Columns(1).Width = 1500
.Columns(2).Width = 2500
.Columns(3).Width = 2000
.Columns(4).Width = 1200
.Columns(5).Width = 1100
.Columns(5).Caption = "Unit Cost" 'Set caption of column 8
.Columns(6).Width = 1200
.Columns(6).Caption = "Total Cost"

End With


'Formatting DataStock (DataGrid)
With DataStock
.Columns(0).Width = 1500 'Setting width for first column
.Columns(1).Width = 2000
.Columns(2).Width = 1500
.Columns(3).Width = 2500
.Columns(4).Width = 1800
.Columns(5).Width = 600
.Columns(6).Width = 600
.Columns(7).Width = 1100
.Columns(8).Width = 1100
.Columns(8).Caption = "Unit Cost" 'Set caption of column 8
.Columns(9).Width = 1200
.Columns(9).Caption = "Total Cost"
End With
```

264

End Sub

'Add item brand to combo box

Private Sub Timer1_Timer()

Dim i, j As Integer
Do Until i = ComboBrand.ListCount
For j = 1 To ComboBrand.ListCount - i - 1
If ComboBrand.List(j + i) = ComboBrand.List(i) Then
ComboBrand.RemoveItem j + i
End If
Next
i = i + 1
Loop

End Sub

Private Sub Timer2_Timer()

'Add category to combo box
Dim i, j As Integer
Do Until i = ComboCategory.ListCount
For j = 1 To ComboCategory.ListCount - i - 1
If ComboCategory.List(j + i) = ComboCategory.List(i) Then
ComboCategory.RemoveItem j + i ' To remove duplicated items
End If
Next
i = i + 1
Loop

End Sub
Private Sub Timer3_Timer()

Timer1.Enabled = False
Timer2.Enabled = False
Timer3.Enabled = False

End Sub

Private Sub Timer4_Timer()
'To add items to Ado Stock
AdoStock.Recordset.AddNew
AdoStock.Recordset.Fields("Date") = Format(Date, "dd/mm/yyyy")
AdoStock.Recordset.Fields("Category") =
AdoInventory.Recordset.Fields("Category")
AdoStock.Recordset.Fields("Brand") =
AdoInventory.Recordset.Fields("Brand")
AdoStock.Recordset.Fields("Item Description") =
AdoInventory.Recordset.Fields("Item Description")
AdoStock.Recordset.Fields("Model Number") =
AdoInventory.Recordset.Fields("Model Number")
AdoStock.Recordset.Fields("CPU") =
AdoInventory.Recordset.Fields("CPU")
AdoStock.Recordset.Update
Timer4.Enabled = False

End Sub

8. Internet Applications
8.1 Web Browser

If you are bored with your existing web browsers, you might want to create your very own web browser using Visual Basic. To create the web browser, you have to press Ctrl+T to open up the components window and select **Microsoft Internet Control**. After you have selected the control, you will see the control appear in the toolbox as a small globe. To insert the Microsoft Internet Control into the form, just drag the globe into the form and a white rectangle will appear in the form. You can resize this control as you wish. This control is given the default name **WebBrowser1**.

To design the interface, you need to insert one combo box which will be used to display the URLs. In addition, you need to insert a few images which will function as command buttons for the user to navigate the Internet; they are the **Go** command button, the **Back** command button, the **Forward** command button, the **Refresh** command button and the **Home** command button. You can put in the command buttons instead of the images but using images will definitely improve the look of the browser.

The procedures for all the commands are relatively easy to write. There are many methods, events, and properties associated with the web browser but you need to know just a few of them to come up with a functional Internet browser. They are listed in Table 8.1.

Table 8.1

Method	Description
GoBack	To navigate backward one page in the history list.
GoForward	To navigate forward one page in the history list.
GoHome	To navigate to the default start page.
GoSearch	To navigate to the current search page.
Navigate	To navigate to the URL or to the file identified by a full path.
Refresh	To reload the file that is currently loaded.
Stop	To cancel the current web page loading operation.
Properties	
Busy	To indicate whether the web browser is engaged in navigation or downloading operations.
LocationName	To retrieve the name of the document that Internet Explorer is currently displaying.
LocationURL	To retrieve the URL of the web page that Internet Explorer is currently displaying.
Event	
DocumentComplete	Executed when a document has been completely loaded.

DownloadBegin	Executed when a navigation operation begins.
DownloadComplete	Executed when a navigation operation finishes.
FileDownload	Executed to indicate that a file download is about to occur.
NavigateComplete	Executed after navigation to a link is completed.

The method navigate is to go the website specified by its Uniform Resource Locator (URL). The syntax is **WebBrowser1.Navigate ("URL").** In this program, if you want to load **www.vbtutor.net** web page at start-up, you can enter this address in the URL slot. The code is

```
Private Sub Form_Load()

WebBrowser1.Navigate ("http://www.vbtutor.net")

End Sub
```

To show the URL in the combo box and also to display the page title at the form caption after the page is completely loaded, we can use the following statements:

```
Private Sub WebBrowser1_DocumentComplete (ByVal pDisp As
Object, URL As Variant)

Combo1.Text = URL

Form1.Caption = WebBrowser1.LocationName

Combo1.AddItem URL

End Sub
```

269

The following procedure will tell the user to wait while the page is loading.

```
Private Sub WebBrowser1_DownloadBegin ()

Combo1.Text = "Page loading, please wait"

End Sub
```

The Code

```
Private Sub Form_Load ()

WebBrowser1.Navigate ("http://www.vbtutor.net")

End Sub

Private Sub Image1_Click ()

WebBrowser1.GoHome

End Sub

Private Sub Image2_Click ()

On Error Resume Next

WebBrowser1.GoForward

End Sub

Private Sub Image3_Click ()

On Error Resume Next

WebBrowser1.GoBack

End Sub

Private Sub Image4_Click ()

WebBrowser1.Refresh

End Sub
```

```
Private Sub Image5_Click ()
WebBrowser1.Stop
End Sub

Private Sub Label2_Click ()
WebBrowser1.Navigate (Combo1.Text)
End Sub

Private Sub Label4_Click ()
WebBrowser1.GoSearch
End Sub

Private Sub WebBrowser1_DocumentComplete(ByVal pDisp As Object,
URL As Variant)
Combo1.Text = URL
Form1.Caption = WebBrowser1.LocationName
Combo1.AddItem URL
End Sub

Private Sub WebBrowser1_DownloadBegin()
Combo1.Text = "Page loading, please wait"
End Sub
```

The Interface is shown in Figure 8.1.

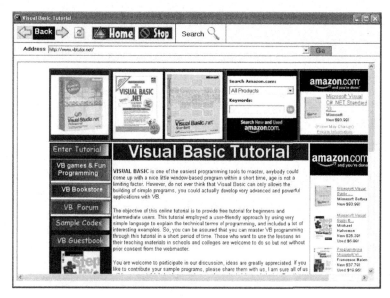

Figure 8.1

8.2 FTP Program

File Transfer Protocol (FTP) is a system for transferring files between two computers over the Internet where one of the computers is known as the server and the other one as the client. FTP program is very useful for website management as it allows the webmaster to update web pages by uploading local files to the web server easily . For normal PC users, FTP program can also be used to download files from many FTP sites that offer a lot of useful stuffs such as free software, free games, product information, applications, tools, utilities, drivers, fixes and etc.

FTP program usually comprises an interface that shows the directories of the local computer and the remote server. Files can be transferred just by clicking the relevant arrows. To log into the FTP site, you have to enter the username and the password; however, for public domains, you just need to type the word anonymous as the username and you can leave out the password. The FTP host name takes the form ftp.servername.com, for example, the Microsoft FTP site's host name is ftp.microsoft.com . FTP program usually provides a set of commands such as ChgDir (changing directory), MkDir (Changing directory), Rename (renaming a file), view (to view a file), delete (to delete a file) etc.

If you need to use a FTP program, you can purchase one or you can download a couple of the programs that are available free of charge over the Internet. However, you can also create your very own FTP program with Visual Basic. Visual Basic allows you to build a fully functionally FTP program which may be just as good as the commercial FTP programs. The engine behind it is **Microsoft Internet Transfer Control 6.0** in which you need to insert into the form before you can create the FTP program. The name of the Microsoft Internet Transfer Control 6.0.is **Inet** and if you only put in one control, its name is **Inet1.**

Inet1 comprises three important properties namely **Inet1.URL** which is used to identify the FTP hostname, **Inet1.UserName** which is used to accept the username and the **Inet1.Password** which is used to accept the user's passwords. The statements for the program to read the hostname of the server, the username and the password entered into the TxtURL textbox, the TxtUserName textbox and the TxtPassword textbox by the user are shown below:

Inet1.URL=Text1.Text

Inet1.UserName=Text2.Text

Inet1.Passoword=Text3.Text

After the user enters the above information, the program will attempt to connect to the server using the following command, where **Execute** is the method and DIR is the FTP command that will read the list of files from the specified directory of the remote computer and you need to use the **getChunk** method to actually retrieve the directory's information.

Inet1.Execute, "DIR"

After connecting to the server, you can choose the file to download from the remote computer by using the statement

Inet1.Execute, , "get" & remotefile & localfile

Where **remotefile** is the file of the remote site and **localfile** is the file of the local system. However, very often you need to provide the full path of the local file, which you can do that by modifying the above syntax to the following syntax:

Inet1.Execute , , "get" & remotefile & localpath & remotefile

The above statements will ensure that the remote file will be downloaded to the location specified by the localpath and the file downloaded will assume the same name as the remote file. For

example, the remote file is **readme.txt** and the localpath is **C:\temp**
, so the downloaded file will be saved in **C:\temp\readme.txt.**

To monitor the status of the connection, you can use the
StateChanged event that is associated with Inet1 together with a set
of the state constants that are listed in Table 8.2.

Table 8.2

Constant	Value	Description
icHostResolvingHost	1	The control is looking up the IP address of the specified host computer.
icHostResolved	2	The control successfully found the IP address of the specified host computer.
icConnecting	3	The control is connecting to the host computer.
icConnected	4	The control successfully connected to the host computer.
icRequesting	5	The control is sending a request to the host computer.
icRequestSent	6	The control successfully sent the request.
icReceivingResponse	7	The control is receiving a response from the host computer.
icResponseReceived	8	The control successfully received a response from the host computer.
icDisconnecting	9	The control is disconnecting from the host computer.

icDisconnected	10	The control successfully disconnected from the host computer.
icError	11	An error occurred in communicating with the host computer.
icResponseCompleted	12	The request has been completed and all data has been received.

Under the **StateChanged** event, you can use the Select Case…End Select statements to notify the users regarding the various states of the connection. The procedure is as follows:

Private Sub Inet1_StateChanged(ByVal State As Integer)

Select Case State

Case icError

MsgBox Inet1.ResponseInfo, , "File failed to transfer"

Case icResolvingHost

Label6.Caption = "Resolving Host"

Case icHostResolved

Label6.Caption = "Host Resolved"

Case icConnecting

Label6.Caption = "Connecting Host"

Case icConnected

Label6.Caption = "Host connected"

Case icReceivingResponse

Label6.Caption = "Receiving Response"

Case icResponseReceived

```
Label6.Caption = "Got Response"

Case icResponseCompleted

Dim data1 As String

Dim data2 As String

MsgBox "Download Completed"

End Select

End Sub
```

The states of the connection will be displayed on Label6.

The FTP program also contains a form and a dialog box. The dialog box can be added by clicking on the Project item on the menu bar and then selecting the Add Form item on the drop-down list. You can either choose a normal dialog box or a login dialog box. The function of the dialog box is to accept the FTP address, the username, and the password and then to establish connection to the server. After a successful login, the dialog box will be hidden, and the main form will be presented to the user to browse the remote directory and to choose certain files to download.

The interface of the login dialog is shown in following figure:

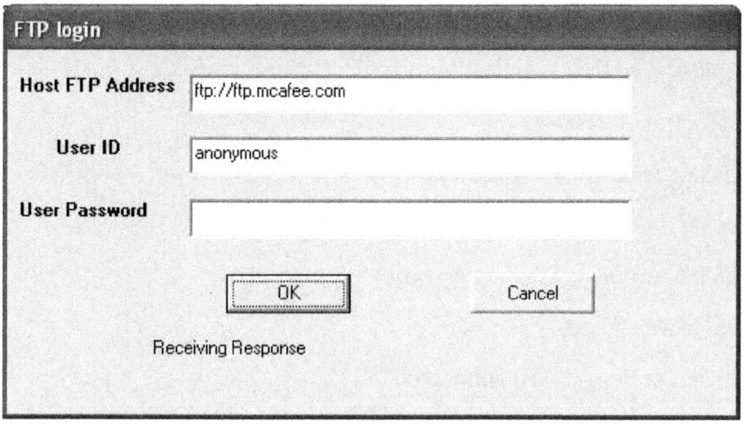

Figure 8.2

The states of the connection will be displayed on the label at the bottom. The program for the login dialog is:

```
Option Explicit

Private Sub OKButton_Click()

Inet1.URL = Text1.Text

Inet1.UserName = Text2.Text

Inet1.Password = Text3.Text

Inet1.Execute , "DIR"

Form1.Show

Dialog.Hide

End Sub


Private Sub Inet1_StateChanged(ByVal State As Integer)

Select Case State

Case icError

MsgBox Inet1.ResponseInfo, , "File failed to transfer"
```

```vb
Case icResolvingHost

Label6.Caption = "Resolving Host"

Case icHostResolved

Label6.Caption = "Host Resolved"

Case icConnecting

Label6.Caption = "Connecting Host"

Case icConnected

Label6.Caption = "Host connected"

Case icReceivingResponse

Label6.Caption = "Receiving Response"

Case icResponseReceived

Label6.Caption = "Got Response"

Case icResponseCompleted

Dim data As String

Dim data1 As String


MsgBox "Transfer Completed"
 Do

        data1 = Inet1.GetChunk(1024, icString)

        data = data & data1


        Loop While Len(data1) <> 0

        Form1.Text6.Text = data

End Select

End Sub

Private Sub CancelButton_Click()
```

279

```
Text1.Text = ""

Text2.Text = ""

Text3.Text = ""

End Sub
```

The statement **data1 = Inet1.GetChunk (1024, icString)** is to use the getChunk method to grab information of the remote directory and then display the files of the directory in the Text6 textbox.

After successful log in, the main form will be presented as shown in the following Figure 8.4.

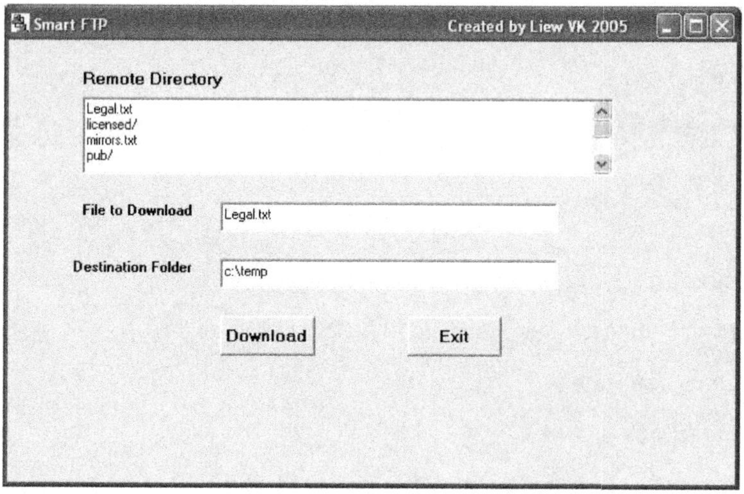

Figure 8.4

The program code to download the file is:

```vb
Dim remotefile As String
Dim mypath As String
Dim cmd As String
Private Sub Command1_Click ()
remotefile = Text4.Text
mypath = Text5.Text
cmd = "GET " & remotefile & " " & mypath & remotefile
Inet1.Execute , cmd
End Sub
Private Sub Command2_Click ()
Inet1.Cancel
End
End Sub
Private Sub Form_Load ()
Dialog.Show
Form1.Hide
End Sub
Private Sub Inet1_StateChanged (ByVal State As Integer)
Select Case State
Case icError
MsgBox Inet1.ResponseInfo, , "File failed to transfer"
Case icResponseCompleted
MsgBox "Download Completed"
End Select
End Sub
```

Index

Abs, 195, 196, 199

Activate, 176

ActiveX data object, 224

AddItem method, 131

ADO control, 224, 227, 230, 234, 235

ADO data controls, 248

array, 71, 75, 115, 193

arrays, 39, 71, 97

ASCII, 34

Atn, 144, 145

avi, 173, 185, 186, 187

Back command, 266

boggle, 111

Boolean, 39, 41, 97, 99, 119, 197, 204

calculator, 193

caption, 115, 220, 224, 268

CD player, 178

check box, 214

chr, 111

Chr, 111

Chr function, 34

Cls method, 204

code window, 116

combo box, 266, 268

Combo Box, 178

command button, 116, 222, 234, 235, 237

common dialog box, 167, 168, 169, 170

components, 173, 224, 266

ConnectionString, 227

controls, 114, 178, 179, 185, 225

data control, 220, 222, 224, 227

database, 220, 222, 223, 224, 227, 229, 236

DatabaseName, 220

DataField, 220, 226

DataGrid controls, 248

DataSource, 220, 226

degree, 2

dialog box, 173, 224, 227, 228, 276

DirListBox, 167, 178, 179, 185

Do Until, 238

Do.... Loop Until, 131

Do...Loop While, 129

DocumentComplete, 267, 268, 270

DownloadBegin, 268, 269, 270

DownloadComplete, 268

dragdrop method, 40

DriveListBox, 167, 178, 179, 185

Elself, 133

End Select, 115, 116, 120, 121, 122, 123, 124, 275, 278

error handling, 216

Exit Sub, 189, 230, 231, 238

FileDownload, 268

FileListBox, 167, 178, 179, 185

FillStyle, 1, 4, 164

FleGrid, 248

For....Next Loop, 127

For...Next loop, 71

For...Next, 72

form, 173, 178, 185, 220, 224, 227, 233, 234, 236, 237, 238, 266, 268, 272, 276, 279

Forward command, 266

FTP, 272, 273, 276

function, 118, 178, 185, 266, 276

getChunk method, 273, 279

Go command, 266

graphics, 224

Home command, 266

icConnected, 274, 275, 278

icConnecting, 274, 275, 278

icDisconnected, 275

icDisconnecting, 274

icError, 275, 277, 280

icHostResolved, 274, 275, 278

icHostResolvingHost, 274

icReceivingResponse, 274, 275, 278

icRequesting, 274

icRequestSent, 274

icResponseCompleted, 275, 276, 278, 280

icResponseReceived, 274, 275, 278

If...Then, 39

image control, 39, 96, 97, 168, 169, 170

Inet1, 272, 273, 274, 275, 277, 278, 279, 280

Int, 75, 76, 111, 116, 122

Integer, 75, 78, 115, 118, 119, 120, 193, 194, 197, 200, 201, 275, 277, 280 interface, 71, 74, 193, 222, 224, 234, 266, 272, 276

interval value, 33, 203

KeyPress, 118

Label, 226

Label controls, 71

list box, 179, 185

List Box, 179

ListIndex, 180, 181, 182, 183, 186, 187, 188

LoadPicture, 12

localfile, 273

LocationName, 267, 268, 270

LocationURL, 267

Loop While, 278

MaxButton, 203

Microsoft ActiveX Data Control 6, 224

Microsoft Internet Control, 266

Microsoft Internet Transfer Control 6.0, 272

Microsoft Jet 3.51 OLE DB provider, 228

Microsoft Multimedia Control, 173, 175, 178, 180, 181, 185

Microsoft Multimedia Control 6.0, 6, 107

midi files, 173, 178, 180

Mod, 127, 128

Move, 73, 74, 75, 79, 80, 81, 82, 83, 84, 85, 88, 89, 91, 92, 150, 221, 222

mp3, 173, 185, 186, 187

mpeg, 173, 185, 186, 187

multimedia files, 173, 180

NavigateComplete, 268

On Error Goto, 216

Option Base, 75

option buttons, 114, 115

password, 33, 34, 35, 36, 37, 38, 106, 107, 133, 232, 236, 238, 272, 273, 276

PasswordChar, 234, 235, 237

PasswordChar property, 133

picture box, 138, 147, 163, 167, 169, 170, 185, 204

Pmt, 159, 161

properties, 72, 175, 220, 225, 227, 233, 234, 237, 266, 273

Pset, 138, 147

randomization process, 75

randomize, 116

RecordSource, 220, 229, 241, 242, 243, 244, 249, 250, 256, 257, 262

Refresh command, 266

remotefile, 273, 280

Rnd, 111

Rnd function, 1, 12, 34, 107, 111

Round, 125, 126, 136, 140, 143, 152

rounded square, 74

runtime, 224

SearchSrting, 242

SELECT, 241, 242, 243, 244, 248, 249, 250, 256, 257, 262

Select Case, 26, 39, 42, 45, 46, 48, 50, 52, 54, 56, 58, 60, 62, 64, 115, 116, 120, 121, 122, 123, 129, 130, 275, 277, 280

shape control, 71

Single, 75

Slot machine, 1

SQL, 232, 241, 242, 248, 249, 250, 256

Sqr, 125, 126, 136, 142, 143, 201

statements, 115, 116, 118, 179, 185, 196, 268, 273, 275

Str, 10, 15, 16, 19, 69, 90, 95, 107, 121, 123, 124, 133,

145, 161, 193, 195, 196, 197, 198, 199, 201, 249, 253, 255, 256, 259, 260, 261

stretchable property, 168, 170

syntax, 268, 273

Timer, 3, 8, 10, 12, 17, 32, 33, 37, 38, 74, 76, 79, 90, 92, 95, 107, 122, 150, 203, 211, 264, 265

timer control, 107, 203

Toolbox, 6, 107

twips, 72

Uniform Resource Locator, 268

URL, 267, 268, 270, 273, 277

Val, 121, 123, 124, 197

variables, 71

Variant, 75, 197, 268, 270

vbCrLf, 216, 217, 218

vbYes, 231

vbYesNo, 231

video files, 173, 180, 185

Visual Data Manager, 247

wav, 85, 86, 173, 180, 181, 182, 185, 186, 187

wave audio files, 180

web browser, 266, 267, 272

Printed in Great Britain
by Amazon